THE IS MANAGEMENT AND BUSINESS CHANGE GUIDES

HOW TO MANAGE SERVICE ACQUISITION

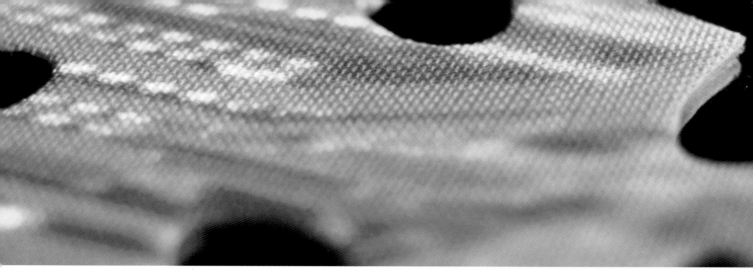

HOW TO MANAGE

Service

Acquisition

FORMAT
PUBLISHING

Published by
Format Publishing Limited
9-10 Redwell Street
Norwich
Norfolk NR2 4SN
United Kingdom

General enquiries/telephone orders: **01603 766544**
Fax orders: **01603 761491**
Email: **sales@formatpublishing.co.uk**
Online ordering: **www.formatpublishing.co.uk**

Edited, designed and typeset by **Format Information Design**

Published for the Office of Government Commerce
under licence from the Controller of Her Majesty's Stationery Office.

First published 2002
ISBN 190309111X

For further information about this and other OGC products, please contact:
OGC Service Desk
Rosebery Court
St Andrews Business Park
Norwich NR7 0HS

Telephone: 0845 000 4999
Email: info@ogc.gsi.gov.uk
Website: www.ogc.gov.uk

Printed in the United Kingdom for Format Publishing

Contents

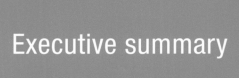

Executive summary

Few organisations can do everything themselves. For those services that are costly, risky or impractical to provide in-house, they turn to outside providers. Acquiring services can bring economy, flexibility and innovation, but also the risk of inefficiency and increased cost. The process of acquiring services must be managed to ensure that strategic goals are realised and that value for money is obtained.

The process of acquisition

There is more to acquisition than selecting a provider and offering a contract. The full process encompasses:

- **origins**: strategic aims and objectives that give rise to the business need for an acquisition

- **requirements**: investigating options for meeting the business need

- **pre-procurement**: scoping the requirement, choosing the sourcing option, and producing a firm specification

- **procurement**: advertising, selection and evaluation of providers, and award of contract

- **implementation and transition**: preparing for the new service and bringing it on-stream

- **making it work**: maintaining the contract and the relationship between client and provider

- **recompetition**: what happens at the end of the contract.

Origins

The acquisition process has its origins in strategy, and must be aligned with it from start to finish. Acquisition begins with the identification of a business need that can be met by acquiring a service; meeting this need should deliver an outcome that is part of the organisation's high-level strategy.

In the early stages it is important to concentrate on meeting business needs, rather than possible sourcing options or particular providers. Focus on what you should do, rather than what you could do. The desired outcomes must be clear at the outset and remain so throughout the acquisition process; everyone involved must know and understand them. Where there is a mismatch between the deal and its objectives, the risk of failure is high.

As well as considering the business needs to be met, these early stages can involve some thought on possible business models, particularly if the business need is radically new or particularly complex. Choosing a business model means deciding at the most basic level how the new arrangement will work and how the private sector will be involved. This might include factors such as delivery methods, charging mechanisms, incentives for providers to invest or to improve quality, and the basis on which the service will be funded, perhaps through a Private Finance Initiative (PFI) deal.

Another way of analysing a potential acquisition is through investment appraisal, where the potential benefits are weighed against costs and risks. Where the acquisition is large or complex, the organisation must be sure that the potential benefits outweigh the costs and risks that will be undertaken. A further dimension is added by sensitivity analysis, which is about asking 'what if?' – what if workloads increase, technology changes, key staff move on, and so on. Not everything can be foreseen, but ensuring flexibility to meet future needs is key when, for example, a long-term partnership is a possibility.

Requirements

Building on a strategic foundation, you can move forward to assessing requirements. Having identified the business needs to be met, you can consider the service or services that will meet them. Finally, the requirement, on which providers will base their bids, is produced.

It is also important to think about how performance will be measured once the contract is awarded – that is, how you will know that the acquisition has been successful.

There will inevitably be some constraints on the acquisition, such as EC procurement rules, internal policies, the needs of business partners or other organisations and shared networks.

A key point is that the requirement should be expressed in terms of what is needed, not how it will be achieved. Too much practical detail could constrain innovation in the solutions that providers offer.

Pre-procurement

Before choosing a provider, consider what kind of arrangement you are seeking. It may be that earlier thoughts on possible business models have already led to a decision; if not, the sourcing option must be decided before procurement begins. The options are in-house provision, short-term (tactical) outsourcing and strategic outsourcing (partnerships). Within these categories there are many possibilities, such as framework contracts with more than one provider or an agreement with a prime contractor who subcontracts components of the service.

Tactical outsourcing is suitable for short-term requirements where the emphasis is on cost-effectiveness rather than building a relationship. Strategic outsourcing is more appropriate for complex, long-term requirements of strategic importance to the organisation. In considering each approach, you should look at its possible benefits, the potential it offers for transferring risk to the private sector, the predictability of demand for the service involved, and the relevant technical factors.

Where the scope and nature of an acquisition are innovative or unusual, it is worthwhile sounding out the marketplace before starting the formal procurement process. Careful use of market sounding can give a useful insight into private sector perspectives early on, helping to refine the requirement and ensuring that the objectives are sound.

Procurement

Procurement is the formal process of choosing a suitable provider and constructing a deal with them. At the outset and throughout this process, the objectives for the acquisition must be kept in mind; it is easy to lose sight of them amid the detail of formal procurement. Requirements should be kept open-ended as far as possible; it may be necessary to rethink the substance of what is needed, although the objectives and desired outcomes will not change.

Procurement begins with the placing of a notice in the OJEC (Official Journal of the European Community) advertising the requirement. From the responses, a selection of providers is chosen who will be invited to tender. (Under the Open procedure, all providers who respond are invited to tender; under the Negotiated procedure, a selection of providers is approached directly.) Selection is about asking of each provider 'can we do business with this provider?' A range of criteria will come into play; they can be divided into financial and non-financial factors (which may be further divided into quantifiable 'hard' aspects or 'soft' aspects that are difficult to measure). 'Soft' factors should not be neglected: cultural fit and the potential benefits of working with a provider are just as important as their technical ability and track record.

When the selected providers have submitted tenders, these are evaluated to decide where the contract will be awarded. Again, evaluation criteria fall into financial, and non-financial categories. Financial criteria must take into account the whole-life costs of the contract. Non-financial criteria include considerations of quality, culture, innovation and risk management.

The prime concern is not cost alone but value for money: the optimum combination of whole-life cost and quality to meet the requirement. To ensure value for money, both financial and non-financial strands of evaluation should be considered separately and then brought together before a decision is made. The final judgement between financial and non-financial aspects must be a major business judgement made by the management board, taking into account key considerations such as affordability and opportunity costs. It will not be possible or appropriate to rely on a mechanistic approach that employs an arithmetical weighting of financial and non-financial factors.

When a provider has been selected, a contract is offered and the agreement formalised. This means translating the mechanisms, features, risks, behaviours and skills that will be involved in providing the service into commercial arrangements, contract terms and management processes. The ability to cope with change over the life of the contract is a key factor.

Implementation

Implementation means bringing the service on-stream and preparing for this event. It is hard work, and requires rigorous management and adequate resources. Ideally, plans for implementation would form part of the contract.

Readiness for a new service touches on many areas. Staff in both organisations must know and understand their new responsibilities. The public (or other end users) must be made aware of the new service and be able to find out more; they must also understand why the new arrangement is better and perhaps be offered incentives to use it. Service management, benefits management and performance measurement processes must all be in place. Finally, contingency plans should be prepared in case of problems, either with the provider failing to deliver or slow uptake of the service.

Making it work

After contract award, keeping everything running smoothly means managing the contract – formal governance – and managing the relationship – ensuring that the parties can work together.

Contract management is about ensuring that both parties meet their obligations to deliver the required objectives and give value for money. If everything is going well, the arrangements will be satisfactory to both parties, with all the anticipated benefits being realised and disputes dealt with to mutual satisfaction – in short, there will be no surprises. The key to good contract management is communication – at all levels, and on a consistent, formalised basis.

Managing the relationship is about building the attitudes and behaviours that encourage mutual success. In major service contracts, which will involve a high degree of interdependence and commitment, a good relationship is crucial to success. Again, communication is paramount, as is the ability to accommodate change.

Recompetition

Recompetition is the process of exiting from an existing contract and creating a new one. The larger and more complex the contract, the more attention needs to be paid to recompetition. Recompetition should be considered before contract award as well as towards the end of the contract term; an exit strategy should form part of the agreement.

Recompetition is both necessary and desirable; it provides opportunities to improve value and quality of service, seek innovation, add flexibility and re-evaluate needs. Organisations must face up to it early and not underestimate the challenges involved.

Planning recompetition will follow a similar process to the original procurement, but with the benefit of experience and lessons learned. Business need should be reassessed and the sourcing option re-examined. The key decision is then whether to retain, split, broaden or completely rethink the scope of the contract. It may also be relevant to consider using more than one provider in place of a single provider, or move towards a different kind of arrangement, perhaps a partnership.

The handover to the new provider needs to be carefully planned; a sound exit strategy will help to reduce the potentially overwhelming advantage of the incumbent provider. This strategy will need to cover such issues as staff and skills, physical assets, intellectual property and data, with the central aim of ensuring business continuity.

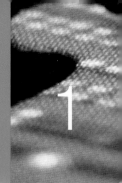

Introduction

1.1 Overview

Few organisations can do everything themselves. Whatever the size and nature of your organisation, there will almost certainly be services that are costly, risky or impractical for you to provide in-house. For these you may turn to outside providers, freeing your organisation from a host of practical concerns and opening it up to the benefits of economy, flexibility and innovation.

But acquiring services also brings the potential for inefficiency, increased cost and unnecessary limitations for your business. This guide can help you avoid the pitfalls and manage the acquisition of services to obtain the maximum benefits for your organisation.

This guidance particularly focuses on the acquisition of IT-related services. With the demands of the Information Age, IT services are often prime candidates for assigning to outside providers. They will almost always be an integral part of business services, and in today's public sector these business services are likely to include some element of electronic service delivery to the citizen. Several organisations may be collaborating to deliver services and each organisation may be responsible for only a part of the total service. There could be further complexity if, for example, there is a 'virtual' service running across several layers of physical infrastructure, each subject to separate contractual arrangements with a number of providers.

Acquiring the right IT services can be complex and difficult. It involves making appropriate choices to meet business need; the aim is for you to get what you need at an affordable price and, subsequently, for your providers to continue to deliver what you want. Acquisition of IT services will contribute to change in the business, and should be business-focused rather than product-driven.

1.2 Who should read this guide

This guide is primarily intended for public sector managers who are involved in major service acquisition and their advisers, as well as 'intelligent customer' units or equivalents (see section 1.5). In addition, the guidance will be of use to the IT services industry in understanding their customers' expectations, concerns and priorities for acquisition of IT services, as this is the area where customers most often seek advice.

This guide concentrates on the acquisition of major IT-related services, of the kind where the responsibility for infrastructure investment will often be passed to the provider. Therefore, it concentrates on the issues around identifying business need, finding a suitable provider and framing an agreement with them, rather than the practical details of (for example) renewing desktop computer systems. OGC's IT Infrastructure Library (ITIL) will be of more help in these areas; see the further information section at the end of this guide.

1.3 Public sector acquisition trends: rightsourcing

Some private sector companies are now reconsidering their sourcing strategies for business services and the associated IT components. Outsourcing had been the preferred route until recently; today the trend is being reversed to some extent. In the financial sector, for example, there is a shift towards insourcing for strategic services. Organisations are reviewing their policies on whether to 'buy in' or 'contract out' service delivery.

HM Treasury has stated its support for 'rightsourcing' – that is, encouraging public sector organisations to seek the most appropriate sourcing option:

> 'In many cases the best way forward is through new partnerships between the public and private sectors…the key test is what works. We will continue to improve, identify and develop new opportunities and partnerships with both the public and private sectors.
> The Government is committed to taking forward a whole range of public private partnerships. That will of course include PFI (the Private Finance Initiative) but not to the exclusion of other forms of partnership.'
>
> *(From a speech by Chief Secretary to HM Treasury, Alan Milburn MP, February 1999)*

Throughout this guide the emphasis is on external service provision.

Sourcing choices

Sourcing choices are made on the basis of decisions about one or more of the following factors:

- meeting policy initiatives
- achieving more economy
- addressing skills shortage
- achieving flexibility
- achieving better service quality
- shortening the time to market, where appropriate
- achieving business synergy with providers
- transferring risk to providers, where appropriate
- gaining access to technologies/methods

- concentrating on core business

- freeing up resources

- achieving cost predictability

- acquiring value-added services.

In practice, sourcing decisions are not always clear-cut. There could be conflicting priorities – for example, achieving more economy may not be easy if it is important to shorten the time to market; trade-offs may need to be made to identify the optimum sourcing option.

Service delivery could be achieved through partnerships, where the organisation collaborates with one or more partners in the public and private sectors. This is a new way of working for many public sector organisations. It requires a very different approach to procurement, concentrating on achieving a favourable deal for both parties and a subsequent focus on both the relationship and the contract.

Public sector organisations must comply with EC procurement rules; there are also demands of accountability and demonstrable value for money.

1.4 Policy drivers and central government initiatives

There are initiatives that will influence acquisition decisions. For central government these include Modernising Government and the four principles of public service reform, with which all public sector investments should comply:

- a national framework of standards and accountability

- within that framework, devolution of power to frontline professionals, enabling local leaders to innovate and develop new services

- better and more flexible rewards and conditions of service for frontline staff

- more choice for consumers of public services and the ability, if provision falls below acceptable standards, to have an alternative provider.

Local government is being reformed in a series of major initiatives to bring about a much stronger sense of community leadership, seamless service delivery and much improved quality of services. Best Value is a concept that underpins much of this reform, setting the context for local government acquisitions.

For the NHS, the major consideration is its own modernisation agenda. The national strategy, Information for Health, is a programme of radical change. It is intended to provide the people, the resources, the culture and the processes necessary to ensure that healthcare professionals have the information they need to support the delivery of care to individuals and to improve public health. Every NHS acquisition will contribute to the national strategy.

Best practice

Wherever possible, public sector organisations are encouraged to follow proven best practice in their approaches to project management, procurement and ongoing service management. Best practice helps to reduce risk and provide good foundations for improved performance.

Electronic service delivery

Electronic service delivery will play a key role in improving services to the public and making it easier for the citizen to interact with government at all levels. The approach will be to provide the citizen with the best possible range of access to paths, or 'channels', to government. The intention is for public sector service delivery to be 'citizen-centred', taking government to the citizen and adapting the services to the needs of the citizen, rather than requiring the citizen to interact on government's terms. Channel services could be provided by:

- organisations which already act as agents of government, such as the Post Office and some professional groups

- local government organisations, which will be encouraged to incorporate central government information in their public information services

- commercial organisations acting as 'channel providers' through a variety of means, delivering public sector services and value-added services to individuals and businesses.

Increasingly, there is a requirement for public sector organisations to adopt innovative solutions to service delivery whenever possible.

*The business case –
new approaches*

New approaches to the financial justification and development of the business case are being explored. Organisations are being encouraged to ask themselves pragmatic questions about their plans for business change, rather than concentrating solely on a formal investment appraisal. They must be able to give positive responses to the following questions:

- is it achievable?

- is it affordable?

- can we manage it?

- can we achieve value for money?

- have we got senior management commitment?

1.5 Terms used in this guide

Many of the terms used in this guidance have a precise meaning in the public sector in addition to their generally understood meaning. Where this is the case it has been flagged in the text where the term first arises. One possible source of confusion is the many terms relating to acquisition: procurement, purchasing, buying, sourcing and so on.

'Procurement'   OGC defines procurement as the whole lifecycle from identifying business need to the end of a contract, which may involve disposal of an asset and/or recompetition. Within this overall lifecycle of procurement activities there will be a pre-procurement stage when decisions are made about scope, sourcing options and so on. Where the organisation does not already have a suitable provider in place (such as a strategic partnering arrangement) this is typically followed by an external procurement process, which must comply with EC procurement rules. The external process concludes with contract award. The remainder of the procurement lifecycle (the most significant part in terms of spending and achievement of outcomes) is the duration of the contract itself.

'Acquisition'   'Acquisition' is a general term that is often used to mean the procurement lifecycle, especially the stages of pre-procurement and external procurement stages leading up to contract award.

'Intelligent customer'   The term 'intelligent customer' refers to the capability of the customer organisation in understanding both sides of a commercial arrangement: the business requirements of the organisation, the technical details of the service, and the market. This allows dealings with tenderers and providers based on knowledge and mutual understanding. The intelligent customer capability can be fulfilled by either an individual or a number of experts within or outside the the organisation.

'Partnership'   Definitions of terms such as 'partnership', 'managed service' and 'outsourcing' differ greatly. Some care is required when discussing options and speaking to potential providers. It is important to be clear about what is required and not to assume that there is a common understanding. The term 'partnership' has a specific meaning in business law – sharing the profits or losses of a business – that is different from that understood by public sector organisations in the present context. In this guidance, a partnership means a relationship in which the parties work together to achieve the business aims of the customer, within a sound contractual framework.

'OJEC'   'OJEC' refers to the Official Journal of the European Community, where high-value public sector contract notices are published.

1.6 Sources   The guidance has been developed from extensive research into current thinking and practice in both the public and private sectors, drawing on published papers and interviews/studies with a number of leading organisations involved in major change. It builds on the work of special interest groups run by OGC with active participation from major public sector organisations, with the aim of researching and addressing issues relating to IT partnership arrangements and other IS management issues.

The guidance builds on earlier OGC best practice in acquisition, incorporating guidance on the Private Finance Initiative (PFI), with new approaches to investment appraisal and evaluation. It is consistent with HM Treasury's advice on procurement policy and practice.

This guidance also responds to lessons learned and the experiences of real-world practical issues, as reported by consultants in OGC's Consultancy Service and their clients. In addition, it incorporates feedback from contributors to OGC workshops and other review channels. These contributions are acknowledged with thanks.

The process of acquisition

2

There is much more to acquisition than simply selecting a provider and offering a contract. This guide takes you through the whole process of acquiring services and providing good foundations for contract management: assessing business need, procurement, optimising and then managing the contract, and finally the process of recompetition at the close of a contract.

The chapters of this guide correspond to the main stages of the acquisition process, which are as follows:

- **origins:** identification of the intention or need for business change, as an outcome of strategic planning, and consideration of possible business models

- **requirements:** investigating options for meeting the business need

- **pre-procurement:** scoping the boundaries of the requirement, deciding on the sourcing option and procurement strategy, and producing a firm specification

- **procurement:** advertising the requirement, selecting suitable providers, evaluating their bids and finalising a commercial deal with the successful provider

- **implementation and transition:** preparing the organisation for the change and bringing the new service on-stream

- **making it work:** maintaining the contract and the relationship between client and provider so that everything runs smoothly

- **recompetition:** restarting the procurement process at the end of the contract to ensure business continuity, value for money and efficiency.

The process of acquisition is shown in figure 1, with the OGC Gateway Reviews mapped on to the process. The column on the right shows the relevant chapters of this guidance. There is more information on the OGC Gateway Reviews in Annex E.

Figure 1
Acquisition illustrated as a
linear process

With acquisition beginning at the top, the parallel processes shown here are the six Gateway Reviews,
the stages of the procurement lifecycle, risk and benefit aspects, and the relevant sections of this
guide to each stage

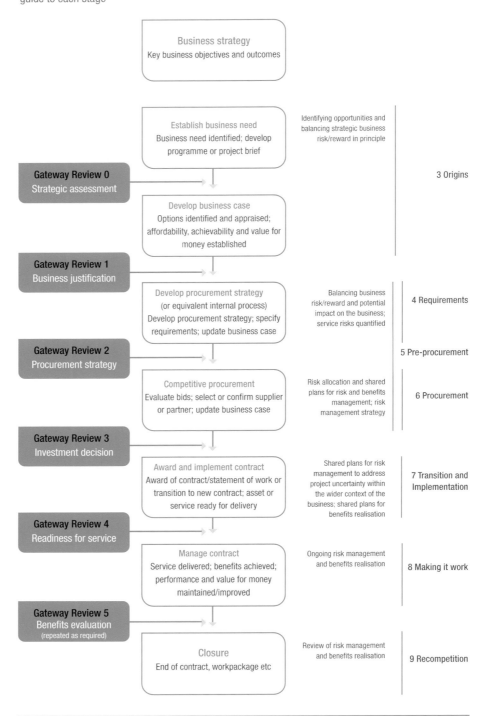

Although it can be helpful to think through acquisition in this linear, step-by-step way, and this is the way this guidance is arranged, in practice the process will be iterative and many issues must be considered in parallel. For example, the process of developing the three stages of the business case (see section 3.5) continues until contract award. Your idea of what you require from the procurement may change, meaning that you have to return to your requirements definition. And although the contract is a formal document that will be awarded to a particular provider (or providers) at a particular point in time, the form it will take and the way in which it will be managed must be considered right from the start.

The main activities that take place in parallel are:

* establishing requirements

* developing the business case

* evaluation and management of costs, benefits and risks

* procurement steps

* contract management considerations.

2.1 Critical success factors

The following factors for successful acquisition are particularly important for partnership arrangements, but equally relevant for acquisition of other sources of external service provision:

* keep sight of the business objectives throughout the process

* demonstrate commitment from the top: senior management should set the right tone in dealings with potential providers

* demonstrate accountability: the senior figure responsible for delivering the requirement of the acquisition should ensure the correct departmental representation on all decision-making bodies and panels

* ensure that procurement advisers are involved from the outset

* seek innovation in thinking about the business model and requirements, as well as in providers' solutions, and be prepared to accept innovative solutions when offered

* recognise that openness is the key to success in complex acquisitions and partnerships; focus on the ongoing relationship with the providers, not the detail of the contract; make processes, evaluation criteria and requirements as transparent as possible to help providers bid realistically

* ensure that requirements are properly scoped and focused on outcomes

* ensure that implementation is adequately resourced

- take a Programme Management approach for acquisition, to ensure that all interdependencies are addressed

- check that contracts match the original or revised requirements and intentions and that contract management issues have been thought through

- build in flexibility and due process for the changes ahead

- ensure that the commercial arrangement continues to meet the organisation's needs, achieves value for money, and remains acceptable to the provider.

Origins

This chapter deals with the origins of the acquisition process. In working through this chapter you are seeking to confirm the business reasons for acquiring a service, and determining whether the direction you intend to take fits with your overall business strategy.

3.1 Focusing on business need

The acquisition process has its roots in the identification of a business need. Meeting this need should deliver one or more objectives of your high-level business strategy. In essence, business need is the understanding that something needs to change (or you want to make a change) in the way you do business – either by moving a service out-of-house or by acquiring a new service from an external provider, or a combination of both.

At this early stage, make sure you genuinely restrict your focus to identifying business needs. You should answer the question 'why?' before you answer the questions 'how?' or 'who?' Focus on what you should do, rather than what you could do.

3.2 Clarity of objectives

A critical factor for establishing a successful deal is to be clear about objectives – not just at the beginning of the process, but throughout it. Objectives are fundamental to a successful deal, but it can be easy to lose sight of them during the procurement process. Objectives for a deal could range from cost reductions to improvements in service delivery and beyond into establishing radically new business models.

Where there is a mismatch between the commercial arrangement you make (or its management) and your objectives, the risk of contract failure is high.

The objectives of the deal need to be clearly articulated, agreed and understood by all stakeholders. The context from which they are derived may be a policy directive, a business strategy, an IT strategy or a business-focused study that identifies a new direction or service delivery requirement for the organisation. Stakeholders may include peer public sector organisations, both central and local government.

Potential opportunities to collaborate with other public sector organisations should not be overlooked. In particular, initiatives such as Modernising Government and the increasing emphasis on joining up public sector services may drive opportunities for joint and collaborative procurement.

Figure 2 shows a cascade model in which objectives or strategies form the origin for the creation of a business model, allow for a successful acquisition and feed into the construction and management of an effective deal.

There is more detailed guidance on managing strategies in the companion guide *How to manage Business and IT Strategies* and more on the reasons (drivers) for change and on benefits management in *How to manage Business Change*.

Figure 2 The cascade model	The cascade model shows the acquisition process beginning in strategy and progressing to a deal through careful consideration of the business model

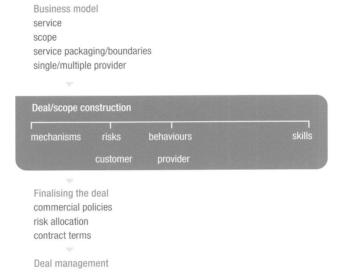

| 3.3 | **The business model** | You will need to determine how you want to work with the private sector within government procurement rules. This means creating a business model – deciding at the most basic level how the new arrangement will work, and on what basis the private sector will be involved. |

How much effort goes into the creation of the business model depends largely on the objectives and strategic importance of the deal. Cost savings will probably require a short-term or fixed price contract, following an established business model. More radical improvement in business performance, or new ways of doing business, are more likely to be achieved through a longer-term strategic relationship.

Are your objectives best delivered by a single provider with end-to-end responsibility, or in a multi-provider environment? There are trade-offs between the risks and benefits of each option – balancing the advantages of a single point of responsibility versus flexibility and potential internal competition and benchmarking.

You will also need to consider the implications for service boundaries – between different providers working together to provide a service, or between provider and public sector organisations.

To create a good business model, it is vital to consider these issues at an early stage:

- who pays: set-up costs, administration costs, transaction costs, and so on; possibilities for a PFI deal or a partnership

- who decides: the basic governance framework that is foreseen for the deal

- what guarantees will be offered to the provider (if any)

- possible payment mechanisms

- incentives for providers to get involved, such as regulated exploitation of commercial opportunities resulting from providing core services

- incentives for providers to improve quality, such as benefits-based charging

- how the deal's success will be defined and measured

- how end users (perhaps the public) will be informed about the service: its existence, benefits, availability, ease of use, timescale, advantages over existing services and so on

- if appropriate, how users will be encouraged to start and continue using the service, including careful considerations of the impact of direct and indirect costs or charges to them for using the service

- how the provider's profit and the organisation's objectives can be aligned and achieved together.

Options for business models range from core infrastructure provision to managed services and/or the complete outsourcing of business processes. Within that scope are many potential packages. Careful consideration of the options can help to create better services for the citizen, delivered in innovative ways, as well as benefits to the organisation.

3.4 Investment appraisal

Investment appraisal is about weighing potential benefits against costs and risks, together with sensitivity analysis.

Benefits are, put simply, the good things that will happen to your organisation if this deal is a success. They are the favourable outcomes that you are hoping your actions will lead to. Certain benefits, such as financial ones, are very easy to measure. Others, such as efficiency or effectiveness, may be more difficult, or even impossible, to define in quantitative terms.

Costs are the financial implications of a course of action – not just the short-term costs of actually paying the provider, but the whole-life costs of the contract. This could mean any cost outside the contract, from needing more staff to manage the contract to the cost of achieving interoperability between different information systems.

Risks are uncertain outcomes; often though not necessarily adverse. Risks can vary greatly in significance and nature, from the risk of complete project or programme failure to the risk of reduced efficiency or increased cost. In order to manage risks, you must first identify them, and this identification is a key part of investment appraisal. The best course of action is not necessarily the least risky: it may be that although some risk is incurred, the long-term benefits justify the risk. In such a case, the techniques of risk management come into play.

Sensitivity analysis is all about asking 'what if?' – what if workloads increase, if technology changes, if key staff move on, if the organisation is restructured. Obviously, not all possibilities can be foreseen, and a plan that is truly ready for every eventuality can only be a theoretical aim. The key is flexibility, and at the very least readiness for those issues that can be foreseen. Other possibilities may be so unlikely that they present only a slight risk to the project.

So investment appraisal consists of weighing these four factors – benefits, costs, risks and possibilities – against each other to assess high-level options. In the public sector, you must carry out your investment appraisal as described in HM Treasury's Green Book.

For more information on managing risk, consult the OGC *Guidelines on Managing Risk*.

3.5 The business case

A business case is a document in which the reasons, advantages and justifications for a possible course of action are set out. It should demonstrate that the proposed approach is achievable, affordable and good value for money, both now and in the future. It is useful not only for focusing thought on the genuine reasons why something needs to be done, but also as a way to demonstrate to senior management why the project should proceed. It is also a valuable planning tool, helping you to manage each stage of the procurement process and ensuring that the decisions made at each stage are informed decisions.

The business case is developed in three progressive stages:

- Strategic outline case: scoping and planning (Initiation)

- Outline business case: indicative assumptions (Feasibility)

- Full business case: validated assumptions (Procurement/Full Study).

The second two stages are reached later on in the acquisition process. At this early stage, your thinking and discussions about high-level business need can usefully feed into the production of a strategic outline case, and help you begin to formulate ideas on your preferred option.

The five case model

Public sector managers of acquisitions are required to produce all three stages of the business case in order to gain management approval for their investments.

It can be constructive to think of the business case (at each of its stages) as being made up of five component cases. These five components – the strategic, economic, project management, commercial and financial cases – are shown below, along with the issues covered in each. At this stage, during the production of the strategic outline case, the considerations will be fairly high-level. Your primary focus will be the business need – that is, asking the question 'why do we need to make this investment?'

- The strategic case – strategic fit, business need and scope

    - the strategic context – fit with the organisation's strategy and related projects, government policy imperatives, existing arrangements

    - need and drivers for change – what is wrong with the status quo?

    - key stakeholders and the nature of their interest in the programme or initiative

    - investment objectives, scope and desired service outcomes

    - constraints

- The economic case – identifying appropriate options

    - wide range of options for meeting the project objectives (including doing nothing)

    - assessment criteria

    - longlisting and shortlisting of options

    - SWOT analysis

- high-level benefit appraisal (financial and non-financial)

- high-level appraisal of costs, where information is available

- high-level analysis of strategic risks

- shortlist of options for more detailed assessment

• The project management case – 'achievability'

- critical success factors

- project management arrangements

- high-level risk assessment and risk management strategy

• The commercial case – the business model and potential deal

- assessment of the likely attractiveness of the project to providers – taking into account the requirements of the Private Finance Initiative (PFI) and Public-Private Partnerships

- assessment of whether the project is suitable for PFI funding

- nature of further work required to sound out the market and inform the procurement process

• The financial case – affordability

- high-level affordability analysis

- ability and willingness of budget holders to meet the resource implications of the project

- statement of support from key stakeholders.

Requirements

4

This section deals with preparing the ground for procurement by determining more specifically what you want from the acquisition and the constraints that act upon your organisation. You will then be in a position to set out the specification and intended outcomes for the acquisition.

Determining requirements forms the basis for all subsequent decisions in the acquisition process and will feed into the construction of the final contract.

4.1 Assessing requirements

Assessing requirements is all about working out what you need: determining what services will be required to realise the desired outcomes from the deal.

Prerequisites

Before you begin assessing your requirements in detail, you should consider these questions:

- do you have a robust business strategy in place, to which this acquisition will contribute?

- if requirements will lead to major change, is your organisation culturally ready to work in new ways?

- is it the right time for this acquisition?

If the answer to any of these is 'no', consider carefully whether you are ready to proceed. You may need to refer to other guidance for help.

Acquiring a major new service, or a step of similar magnitude, can lead to significant business change for your organisation. The companion guide *How to manage Business Change* includes more detail on the issues involved, including guidance on assessing cultural readiness.

The companion guide *How to manage Business and IT Strategies* can help in the formulation and management of high-level strategy.

What outcomes do you want?

Your organisation may be seeking greater effectiveness, improved efficiency, more economy, or a combination of all three. Typically, the required outcomes would be identified as part of earlier business planning, when developing objectives.

In the example overleaf, Organisation X has completed a major review of its relationship with the public. Its high-level outcomes are set out as a vision statement to meet its business objectives.

Desired outcomes in Organisation X's relationship with the public are:

* a 'one-stop-shop' approach for service delivery to the public

* a range of means for service delivery:

    * face-to-face, call centre and website

    * the choices to be determined by the need to balance customer preferences and Organisation X's needs for security and efficiency

    * meeting the needs of citizens who might otherwise be excluded from the Information Age

* multi-functional ways of interacting with the public that reflect sensible and efficient grouping of activities across the range of Organisation X's business and beyond, including flexibility for providing more proactive services to selected groups of citizens on demand

* better access to new information relevant to a range of Organisation X's business activities

* improved use of information already held, with automatic access for staff to all relevant information held on customers, providers and others interacting with Organisation X

* improved public access, increased openness and transparency

* accurate and timely decisions in transactions with the public, with automated and clear explanations of decisions where required

* common definitions and terminology across Organisation X and its partners

* reduced end-to-end time in completing transactions.

Clearly, outcomes of this range would not normally be achieved through one single procurement; typically, this would be a modernisation or improvement programme. In practice, most organisations would conduct a number of procurements that could be interdependent and share a number of common features. A formal Programme Management approach helps to ensure that the organisation can coordinate related activities effectively. For more information on programme management, see the complementary OGC guide *Managing Successful Programmes*.

What services will you need?

Having decided on the required outcomes, you need to decide what services will be needed to realise them. This is about thinking through in detail what providing the service will mean in practice.

Service requirements may include any or all of the following:

- business services with supporting IT, such as a call-centre service

- IT services for the organisation's internal use, such as a range of Intranet-enabled information services delivered direct to the user's desktop

- support for management of change programmes in the organisation

- consultancy support, such as advice on strategy, programme or project management

- application development – for example, development of an application for electronic transactions with customers

- operational services – the provision and maintenance of operational services for users, such as service desk support and application maintenance

- infrastructure, such as extending and updating telecommunications networks and facilities.

There may also be a requirement for the organisation to sell its products or services – perhaps selling information direct to the public.

Depending on the scope of the requirements, it may be appropriate to classify services into broad categories such as the ones summarised above. This helps purchasers to group services together to which similar contract terms and performance measures could be applied. In addition, services may need to be packaged together in ways that make them attractive to the marketplace.

4.2	Producing a specification

Producing a specification means translating your requirements into a formal statement of what is required from the acquisition.

HM Treasury guidelines advise that, to the greatest extent possible, the requirement should be expressed in terms of output and performance to avoid any suggestion of favouritism and to provide scope for innovative solutions. (See the companion guide *How to manage Performance* for more information on outputs and performance.)

Requirement documents come in many forms and under many names – statement of requirement, operational requirement, specification of service requirement, output (based) specification and specification of business requirements.

The document title may indicate the project focus, but the way in which the requirement is expressed is much more important – you should aim to set down what is required rather than how it should be delivered. The intention is to avoid specifying solutions and unnecessary detail and to give providers the flexibility to propose the structures, systems and services to best meet the requirement.

When the intention of the procurement is to establish a long-lasting partnership, the details of the specific service requirement that prompted the procurement exercise may well be less important than the scope of future service deliveries and the requirements for partnership and collaboration. The requirement, in this case, is for a relationship rather than a specific product or service. A specification will still have value, but may well become a minor consideration and should not be allowed to dominate the procurement decision.

Partnership considerations

As you produce a specification it may be helpful to consider whether a partnership arrangement (see section 5.1) is likely. This is because classifying requirements as desirable/not desirable (or mandatory/not mandatory) in a binary way is not the best way to prepare the ground for a partnership. Instead, there may be questions about how a requirement is to be met and at what cost, and the degree of confidence you have in the provider's ability to deliver against that requirement.

Content of a specification

Your high-level business goals should be translated into a requirements specification to meet the stated business needs. To establish the detail, you will need to determine the following:

- the key business processes

- the information flows to support these processes

- what business managers say they want and why, and its relevance to the business

- what process and data owners say they need and why

- how data content and information flows will be used

- the minimum requirements of data and information

- the interaction between processes and functional organisation

- relevant acceptance criteria.

Performance measures need to be developed in parallel, to help you measure whether the subsequent service has achieved what all stakeholders wanted. These are measurable business benefits of effectiveness, efficiency and economy – such as increased customer satisfaction, better support for decision taking and faster response times. See the companion volume *How to manage Performance* for more information.

Purchasers should also be looking at risk – the risks to the business if they proceed with plans (and if they do not go ahead), risks associated with providers and risks associated with different approaches and solutions. Where it is appropriate and cost-effective to do so, purchasers may also be thinking about transferring some risks to providers at this point. (OGC's *Guidelines on Managing Risk* provide detailed information on this topic.)

At the same time, they should be thinking about evaluation criteria – that is, how to determine the providers who are most able to meet the objectives of the requirement.

How much detail?

One approach is to describe the nature of the service in one or two sentences, then break statements down into essential and desirable aspects without implying a need for simple yes/no responses. You should be seeking answers about the ways in which the requirement could be met and indicative costs of different approaches. The specification should go no further than identifying options; it is important to check that providers would not be unduly constrained at this stage.

A specification should be produced in outline before carrying out surveys of the service marketplace. If the industry is approached too early in the development process there is a risk that the solution to the problem is decided before it has been thought through.

Depending on the complexity of the requirement, purchasers may need to call upon the expertise of a range of specialists such as IT experts. Where appropriate, the requirement is developed in consultation with providers advising on the feasibility of the approach. It should be noted that innovative solutions proposed by competing providers must be treated as confidential commercial information.

Procurement staff should always be involved from the beginning; they can advise on a number of issues relating to procurement and procurement law. They will be responsible for developing the contractual clauses to complement the requirement documentation.

There are no fixed rules for structuring specifications, and no single model that could fit every requirement. However, the example specification in Annex A provides a starting point.

A list of useful sources of help is provided at the end of this guide.

4.3 Assessing constraints

There are sure to be some constraints on the scope, content and manner of your acquisition. Constraints for public sector organisations include external factors such as European Monetary Union (EMU), government factors such as legislation affecting public sector organisations, and internal factors that may arise within the organisation such as internal policies and standards. Not all of these constraints will apply to every requirement.

External factors

These are factors that are outside the organisation's control and that everyone has to consider, such as the impact of the European Monetary Union or the Data Protection Act.

Public sector organisations are responsible for ensuring that they comply appropriately with EC procurement rules. They must also demonstrate value for money.

Broadly speaking, sound practice for the pursuit of value for money under appropriate award procedures, and meeting various publicity and information requirements, will ensure compliance with the EC rules and other international obligations.

UK contract and commercial law are additional factors that affect every organisation. In addition, there is other legislation that must be considered. This includes the Data Protection Act and standard policies such as Equal Opportunities and Health and Safety. Procurement advisers should be able to identify the issues relevant to individual circumstances.

Other issues that may need to be considered include:

- the rising expectations of the public

- the impact of new technologies

- the maturity of the IT services marketplace.

Internal factors

Within the organisation there will be additional constraints that may need to be considered. There should be business and IT strategies to which this requirement contributes. There will be internal policies associated with these strategies, concerned with issues such as sourcing and benefits management; there will also be technical policies and standards. And if working with business partners, their strategies and standards may impose constraints. The strategies of customers and providers, as part of a service or supply chain, may also have an impact on plans.

There may be other practical constraints to consider. For example, there may be a need to take account of other projects and programmes going on at the same time (and any dependencies that affect the requirement); the resources available; the timing for implementing the requirement or constraints for existing legacy systems that need to be integrated with current plans.

Shared networks

A number of organisations make extensive use of shared networks. A private sector example is the financial sector's infrastructure; public sector examples include the Government Secure Intranet (GSI), NHSnet and the networks shared by research establishments and academic communities. There are specific technical and security constraints for organisations joining these networks, which may have a significant impact on the feasibility of plans for service delivery – for example, making shared plans much easier to implement or imposing technical constraints on third party providers that must be met. There may also be other issues associated with electronic service delivery, such as a requirement for encryption or digital signatures.

See Annex D for greater detail on the use of standards in a service acquisition.

4.4 Decision point: business justification

This first decision point focuses on the business justification for the acquisition.

There should be a robust business case for the acquisition, demonstrating that it meets business need, is affordable and achievable, and will provide value for money. Where applicable, it should also be established that the acquisition will contribute to wider strategic aims or far-reaching business change.

The requirement specification must be realistic, clear and unambiguous. The constraints acting upon the organisation in general, and applying to this acquisition in particular, should have been taken into account, and the full scale and impact of relevant external issues should have been considered.

Where appropriate, you should also have ensured that the major risks have been identified and outline risk management plans have been developed.

This decision point corresponds with OGC Gateway Review 1 (see Annex E).

Pre-procurement

5

There are many issues to consider before procurement begins, the main one being the choice of sourcing option to support the chosen business model. Before trying to find the actual provider who will be used, it is important to consider what kind of arrangement you are seeking.

At this stage, you should be in a position to say with reasonable confidence what kind of arrangement you are trying to create, having looked at the options and weighed the potential costs, benefits and risks of each one. You will also have considered issues such as the importance of technical factors and whether IT services can usefully be grouped together for procurement purposes.

5.1 Sourcing options

Some options for sourcing are outlined below.

In-house provision

Services may continue to be provided by an internal provider, particularly where the service is regarded as core or where there is a high level of business uncertainty that increases the risks of contracting out. In-house service provision will usually follow an assessment against other options and will be based on some form of internal service level agreement.

Short-term (tactical) outsourcing

Short-term or tactical outsourcing is appropriate when the requirement is for delivery of services on a relatively short-term service-by-service basis, possibly to cover transitions in technology. The emphasis in such cases is likely to be on cost-effectiveness rather than on a long-term relationship.

Strategic outsourcing: partnerships and PFI

Longer-term outsourcing may be said to be strategic because of the nature of the service or contract required. For example, the requirement is for a long-term contractual relationship with a single (or small number of) private sector providers, perhaps covering all services or major services, with the intention of developing a relationship of major importance to the customer organisation.

Such strategic relationships are often referred to as partnerships, especially where there is a degree of risk and reward sharing and mutual interdependence, or where the focus of the relationship is more clearly linked to business improvement rather than just service delivery.

Partnerships are long-term arrangements between public sector bodies and commercial providers aimed at achieving strategic goals. Many such bodies are looking at the scope for more flexible, less adversarial arrangements with service providers, wherever they provide better value.

Partnerships are a new way of working for most public sector organisations and may also be new to the provider. Both parties need to be 'informed partners' in that they understand what each has to do to develop and maintain a productive and mutually beneficial relationship. This shared understanding is the single most important factor in the success or failure of a partnership; both customer and provider must appreciate what the other is hoping to gain from the arrangement.

Partnership models include joint ventures, business synergy, strategic outsourcing, joint resource and the Private Finance Initiative (PFI), where private sector capital investment is sought. A key element of PFI projects is that there must be a significant transfer of risk to the private sector, in return for which the private sector may expect greater control over the delivery process.

Flexible subcontracting arrangements

This recently developed model establishes a clear vertical division between a prime contractor, who is engaged as a strategic partner, and their subcontractors. An illustration of this model is shown in figure 3. The prime contractor is at liberty to effect recompetitions between its subcontractors at any time. This ensures competitive pricing and service provision. In addition, the client organisation can carry out a recompetition for a new prime contractor and leave the subcontracting arrangements in place. This approach has the advantages of increasing competition while at the same time safeguarding business continuity.

5.2 Choosing the sourcing option

The analysis of sourcing options is sometimes dominated by just two options: to do the work in-house or to outsource. However, this may mask the range of choices actually available. For example, is the requirement long-term or short-term, input/resource or service/output focused? Nor are in-house/outsource options mutually exclusive. An in-house team may, for example, buy in additional external resources, expertise and services. The options available will vary, and you must ensure that the approach taken matches your needs at the time. A well-formulated business model (see section 3.3) will eliminate many options from the outset, but there may still be choices to be made.

For each service there may be differing priorities, requirements, risks and opportunities. Considering a range of factors, and how they may interact in relation to a particular service, helps to identify potential conflicts and issues and may prompt management action – to minimise risk, perhaps.

Figure 3
A flexible subcontracting
arrangement

A flexible subcontracting arrangement, with a prime contractor engaged and granted the authority
to change sub-contractors as required. The client organisation can change the prime contractor
and leave the unaffected aspects of the arrangement in place

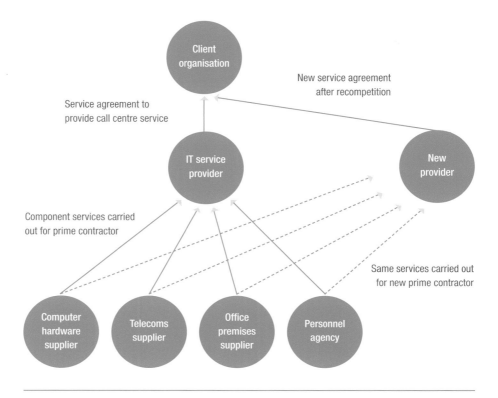

It must be emphasised that there are no general prescriptions. Decisions about
sourcing options require sound business judgement in the context of each
organisation's own circumstances, and re-evaluation of those decisions in the light
of changing circumstances.

Priorities that may affect the choice of sourcing option include:

- **policy:** internal or external policy initiatives dictate a particular route or
  constrain the available options

- **economy:** the organisation is seeking more economical ways of delivering
  services in comparison with what it is doing now and/or what others are
  paying for similar services

- **skills shortage:** the customer organisation lacks the required skills internally
  and must either buy them in or outsource the service

- **flexibility:** the organisation requires the ability to vary its requirement and/or service providers over time

- **service quality benchmarking:** the organisation is seeking improved quality of service in comparison with what it is doing now and/or what others are achieving with similar services

- **time to market:** the length of time taken to develop the requirement, procure and implement the service is a key factor

- **business synergy:** the organisation seeks service providers whose operations will complement its own activities

- **risk transfer:** the organisation seeks to transfer risks to private sector providers if they are better placed to manage them

- **access to technologies/methods:** a primary consideration is access to new ways of doing things and/or new technologies without having to invest internally in keeping up to date

- **core business focus:** the organisation wants to concentrate on its core business and outsource other activities

- **cost predictability:** the organisation's priority is to be able to make accurate forecasts for current and future spending

- **value-added services:** the organisation seeks added value from its service provider.

The following notes give more detail on aspects to consider when making a sourcing decision. The essence of this decision is the weighing against each other of the costs, benefits and risks of the various courses of action open to you.

What kind of services do you need?

Looking at the organisation's requirements in broad terms helps to highlight the appropriateness of different sourcing options. There are two key factors: duration and type of arrangement sought; and whether requirements are 'output' or 'input' orientated. Where requirements can be readily expressed in output or outcome terms, it should be easy to contract for a complete service – passing responsibility for service delivery to the provider. Conversely, there may be requirements for resources that will be deployed under internal management and control – advice on strategy formulation, for example.

Framework contracts that allow customers to call off resources are suitable for meeting an 'as-and-when' requirement for resources, such as for technical assurance, project management and strategic planning. Partnership contracts (see section 5.1) generally seek to establish a long-term relationship with a single provider, which develops over time as new requirements emerge. Customers may wish to retain an element of competition, perhaps by setting up a number of service contracts with other providers and allocating work to whichever provider is performing best at the time.

What are the desired benefits?

The type of benefits being sought is particularly important in assessing sourcing options. For example, is the emphasis on cost savings or on improvements in business value? The latter are more likely to be sought through longer-term strategic contracts. Shorter-term 'commodity' services are more likely to be concerned with short-term cost savings. Business-value driven contracts may include provision to:

- encourage joint initiatives between customer and provider

- seek to share resulting rewards or risk

- allow the service provider to promote and expand, rather than seek to limit, its business within the organisation.

Where costs savings are the main benefit sought, a greater emphasis is likely to be placed on a firm (if short-term) or fixed-price contract. However, public sector organisations must always seek value for money.

Similarly, the nature of the contract management approach is likely to differ. If cost savings are the primary driver, close monitoring and control of the provider is likely to be emphasised, rather than joint investigation and exploitation of new opportunities, with greater formality and an arm's-length relationship emphasised over partnership and mutual trust.

Who will manage the risks?

Certain kinds of procurement may offer the potential for risk transfer – that is, transferring the risks inherent in providing the service to the provider. An example would be an IT infrastructure service agreement where the provider agrees to ensure an agreed level of service, say 95% availability, or perhaps to respond to outages within a stipulated time. Under such an agreement, the client organisation seeks to transfer the risks inherent in IT provision to the provider, rather than managing the risk itself (which in this case would involve responding to each problem as it arose). While this is beneficial to the client, who has more time to concentrate on more strategic issues, there will be costs involved in achieving this 'insurance' against risk.

Under the public sector PFI (Private Finance Initiative) and partnership arrangements, the private sector must genuinely assume risk. This does not mean that all risks should be transferred to the private sector; risks must be allocated to the party best placed to manage them. The aim is for risks to be shared between client and provider in a manner that is fair and agreeable to both parties in the arrangement.

There is more information on the types of risk and how they are managed in the OGC *Guidelines on Managing Risk*.

How strategically important is the service?

It is important to distinguish between services that contribute directly to your organisation's high-level strategies (strategic), and those that facilitate or enable day-to-day business activities (non-strategic). Non-strategic services can be evaluated in a binary way: they either fulfil the requirement or they do not. They need only be done well enough to prevent them becoming a problem. Strategic services are critical and need to be done as well as your organisation knows how. The better they are done, the more benefits will result.

The lower the strategic importance and the lower the relative efficiency and effectiveness of in-house provision, the stronger the case for contracting out. Services such as the IT infrastructure support discussed above may be very costly for the organisation to provide in-house. Keeping them in-house does not provide any great benefit and is unlikely to be seen as particularly desirable by many people in the organisation. Such services are non-strategic; they need to be done well, but no better. Other services, such as knowledge management to support strategic decision-making, have much greater strategic importance, and are unlikely to be entrusted to providers. They need to be done as well as possible for the good of the organisation.

Deciding what makes a service strategically important can be difficult. For public sector organisations, where competitive advantage is rarely an issue, services that ensure the organisation's ability to respond quickly and flexibly to future change may be key.

What might the future bring?

In principle, it may seem that the more predictable the demand for a service, the easier it is to negotiate a sound contract. If demand for a service is not stable, or cannot be forecast with confidence, there could be risks in entering contracts that fail to provide adequate flexibility. However, it is possible to construct a contract that incorporates mechanisms for pricing of variable demand. One of the benefits of outsourcing services is the potential ability of service providers to accommodate variable demand through their economies of scale.

The more tightly the service requirement can be defined and the more certain the future requirement, the less apparent risk. Two possible approaches to managing the risk of unclear future demands are:

- to develop partnership agreements (see section 5.1) where there will be an element of sharing risks and rewards in future

- to put in place some form of call-off arrangement where the customer pays for services as they are required, so minimising commitments whilst providing flexibility.

However, there will be always be risks associated with the ability of the service provider to perform and deliver as required.

Technical factors

Technical factors may, at times, be particularly important in sourcing decisions. They may constrain your options or even conflict with your preferred business options.

Integration is one key factor. The more 'standalone' a service (and the technology that underpins it) is, the more amenable to an independent sourcing route it becomes. If it is highly integrated with other sources, this might be less appropriate. Highly integrated services and systems (for example, a chain of services involving different providers) will be difficult to source separately.

Maturity is another important factor. This concerns the extent to which the underpinning technology and the type of service are mature on the market and/or well understood within your organisation. Unfamiliarity or a low level of maturity may bring difficulties and risks in contracting out, and a need to find ways of mitigating such risks.

See Annex C for a checklist giving greater detail on the issues surrounding sourcing options.

5.3 Grouping IT services

The best sourcing option for one service may not be best for another. Unbundling IT services provision, and approaching IT as a portfolio of systems and services, makes it possible to identify how requirements vary and whether there are different sourcing opportunities.

One of the key factors determining the degree of bundling or unbundling of services is the scale of the resulting contract management task and the complexity of service interfaces. For these reasons, organisations may choose to contract out all of their IT activities to a single provider. Even so, analysis of options is best approached by considering each service in turn, then looking at options for grouping or packaging them.

Some trade-off may be required to package services for the marketplace. If the scope and value of the services offered are too small, companies may decide that it is too expensive to bid. The aim must be to get the right balance to ensure best use of what the market can offer, while meeting the customer organisation's requirements. The sourcing options must be considered in the light of the requirement scope, which may be defined in terms of projects, services, applications, resources, functional domain, geographic area and/or site.

The following points will need to be considered when grouping services:

- the commonality of information, communication requirements and dependencies between services – for example, between the service desk and problem management function

- the customers of the service and the impact of contracting out. For example, would a single point of contact for customer enquiries be lost or would fragmentation of the IT infrastructure impair inter-working?

- technical factors, such as the type of hardware and software used

- the probable response from the market

- the cost of competing IT services

- the locations at which services are delivered.

The grouping of IT services should not:

- include incompatible services which should be managed under separate contracts

- compromise control of, and independence from, the IT provider by the customer. For example, systems development and software quality audit should be grouped separately

- consist of one group of disparate services, thus preventing the customer from selecting the best provider for particular types of services

- result in too many contractors providing services, causing a large management overhead and control problems – for example, difficulties in integrating the many interfaces between organisations

- be too small, creating a poor response from the market and wasted effort for both customer and bidders.

5.4 Market sounding

When the scope and nature of an acquisition are in some way innovative or unusual, it is worthwhile sounding out the marketplace before starting the formal procurement process. Market sounding is not required for all procurements; it is used when you are seeking to achieve business change as a result of the procurement and/or where the likely interest of the market needs to be gauged before going further.

Careful use of market sounding can give a useful insight into private sector perspectives early on. The results of a market sounding exercise should help refine the requirement and the scope of the acquisition to ensure that the market is likely to be willing and able to respond when the procurement begins. Another aim should be to ensure that the scope and objectives are sound and that the decision to go ahead is well founded.

Where the requirement is particularly novel and likely to be unfamiliar to the industry, you may need to, in effect, 'create the market' by providing companies with an opportunity to hear about and explore what the organisation has in mind. This can help providers consider how they may be able to contribute and thereby maximise the prospects for competition.

Whatever form market sounding takes, it is essential to ensure that future competition is not distorted or discriminating as a result of providing potential providers with information that gives them an advantage.

Prior Information Notices (PINs)

Market sounding can take the form of placing a Prior Information Notice (PIN) in the OJEC (Official Journal of the European Community) at the beginning of the financial year. PINs give an outline of the organisation's intended direction for the coming year and its likely procurement needs. This has benefits for both the organisation and its potential providers, as it gives providers time to consider their responses before OJEC advertisements are placed. Potential providers can make contact to discuss opportunities in general terms.

Public sector organisations may need to make both the market and key stakeholders, such as ministers, aware of progress in the high-level plans for business change, perhaps through use of a prospectus or information pack in addition to a PIN. Consideration may also be given to sharing the outline business case with potential providers at this early stage, to allow them a better insight of the business and its priorities.

Because they are general and do not specify requirements in detail, there is a need for balance when drafting PINs. While they should be broad enough to allow for opportunities to extend the boundaries of services to be provided under any subsequent contract, they should also be precise enough to ensure that misleading messages are not sent to the market.

Market sounding checklist

- Test viability of scope/approach

- Assess competition/potential market

- Feed information gained at this stage into scope

- Ensure early sight of your plans for industry – their readiness/consortium building

- Recognise that this is not a selection process

- Ensure 'level playing fields' for all potential providers by giving equal information to all

- Ensure that key messages are conveyed (for example, to assure market that incumbent has not got the certainty of winning).

5.5 Decision point: procurement strategy

This decision point focuses on the strategy for the actual procurement process.

The outline business case can now be created; it should validate the preferred way forward and assess potential value for money, affordability and achievability. You should have a robust and appropriate strategy for procurement that will facilitate a good client/provider relationship both before and after contract award.

You should also confirm that funding is available for the entire service acquisition, including contract management activity, before beginning procurement.

This decision point corresponds with OGC Gateway Review 2 (see Annex E).

Procurement

6

This chapter deals with finding a suitable provider and constructing a suitable deal within which they will provide services to your organisation.

OGC's recommended approach to the formal procurement process (that is, from OJEC advertisement to contract award) is described in OGC's *Procurement Project Guidelines*.

Value for money – the need for business-focused judgement in evaluation

Value for money over the life of the contract depends on achieving the optimum balance of whole life costs and quality to meet the requirement. When evaluating tenders the final judgement between financial and non-financial aspects must be a major business judgement made by the management board, taking into account key considerations such as affordability and opportunity costs. It will not be possible or appropriate to rely on a mechanistic approach that employs an arithmetical weighting of financial and non-financial factors.

6.1 Keeping the objectives in mind

Your objectives for this acquisition will already have been set, and agreed with all stakeholders, before the start of the formal procurement process. Throughout the procurement process, you should refer back to these objectives (for example, at project board or steering committee meetings and in project documentation), to ensure that developments stay in line with objectives.

You may find that you have to revise your thinking on what you need, or how it will be provided, during the procurement. It may prove impossible to obtain what you originally wanted, or an innovative, unforeseen alternative may be offered. The requirement should be kept open-ended for as long as possible, to ensure that opportunities do not have to be ruled out. However, although the requirement or business model may have to change, the objectives for the deal should remain constant.

6.2 Procurement routes

There are three formal options for procurement procedure in the public sector: Open, Restricted, and Negotiated.

- **the Open procedure** requires that all service providers who respond to the contract notice published in the OJEC must be invited to tender. Most service procurements that are suitable for the Open procedure could more efficiently be acquired through catalogues such as Construction Line or the IT-related S-CAT. Such requirements are typically very straightforward, low-risk and well understood by both customer and providers. Catalogues speed up the procurement process by identifying a range of suitable providers on the public sector's behalf, thus saving the time and effort involved in sifting potentially large numbers of provider responses

- **the Restricted procedure** is appropriate where a requirement can be specified in sufficient detail for proposals to be developed by service providers and evaluated by the customer without significant negotiation.

- **the Negotiated procedure** may be more appropriate where the customer organisation seeks an innovative approach from the industry and/or where it is not appropriate (or possible) to specify a detailed requirement in advance.

The Negotiated procedure may only be used in certain circumstances. The derogations for its use are set out in the EC rules.

Whatever procurement route is taken, public sector procurement teams must be able to justify their choice according to EC procurement rules.

6.3   Selection

Selection is about assessing providers: asking the question 'is this a provider with whom we can do business?' The outcome of the selection process is a shortlist of the companies who have proved most suitable for consideration as competitors to provide the required services.

To ensure value for money, both financial and non-financial factors will be included in a set of weighted selection criteria, of which providers should be made aware. Non-financial factors may be 'hard' factors that can be measured in some way – for example, x number of staff available, y number of similar contracts. 'Soft' factors are much more difficult to pin down because typically they address intangible aspects such as culture and compatibility.

'Hard' factors include:

- ability to deliver: skills, efficiency, experience, track record and reliability

- technical capacity: staff, skills, resources, equipment, technology, premises, subcontracting experience and so on

- economic and financial standing: is the provider likely to remain in business and maintain their current core business? Do they have plans for change that could have implications over the life of the contract?

'Soft' factors include:

- cultural fit: could customer and provider achieve a good working relationship? What aspects of relationship management and teamworking are relevant to the business context?

- the potential benefits of working with this provider (including risk transfer, where appropriate)

- approaches to risk allocation and management.

The OGC publication *Supplier Financial Appraisal Guidance* will be useful in assessing the financial status of potential providers.

6.4 Evaluation

Evaluation is about assessing providers' tenders on the basis of economic advantage to the contracting authority.

There must be a formal evaluation process culminating with a report that summarises each evaluation stage, but over-reliance on a paper evaluation of proposals can cause problems. What really matters is the customer's confidence in the provider's proposals, and whether customer and provider together can achieve value for money over the life of the contract.

Evaluation criteria

Let tenderers know what you are going to evaluate against, and the reasons why, and make sure you follow through on what you have said. This openness will smooth the process of evaluation. Within the bounds of commercial confidentiality, be open about your objectives and processes so that providers will be clearer about the reasons for your priorities.

As with selection, the criteria for awarding the contract can be divided into financial, 'hard' (measurable) and 'soft' (difficult to measure) factors. Evaluation criteria should be weighted according to the priorities at hand.

Financial criteria must take into account the whole-life costs of the contract. Some key criteria for financial and 'hard' aspects include:

- business need – ensuring that the bid covers everything that is currently required, to the required quality of service

- providers' plans for implementing the service

- achievability – checking that the provider fully understands the implications of implementing the service and can support this with appropriate plans (this may also apply to the customer organisation)

- robustness of solution

- proposals for implementation/roll-out

- affordability and value for money, balanced with a reasonable return for the provider.

'Soft' or difficult-to-measure criteria could include:

- quality of service offered

- the potential for innovation (and realism about achieving it)

- organisational culture

- risk management

- environmental issues.

Note that confidentiality of commercial information about individual solutions must be protected.

The recommended approach for evaluating tenders to ensure value for money is to evaluate the two strands (financial and non-financial/'hard' and 'soft') separately and then bring them together before making a decision on awarding the contract. Unless the two strands point to the same provider, a decision must be made based on a careful consideration of the risks of the various possible courses of action. This decision should be taken by the management board.

6.5 The contract

Having selected providers to enter the competitive procurement process and determined through evaluation that they meet all the requirements, you must create a commercial agreement that will be satisfactory to both parties for the length of the contract.

This means considering all the mechanisms, features, risks, behaviours and skills that will be involved in providing the service or services and translating them into:

- **commercial arrangements:** for example, on commitment, pricing, benchmarking, indexation, asset ownership and exploitation and risk allocation

- **contract terms:** for example, on duration, change control, dispute resolution, termination and liability

- **management processes:** for example, on joint management and planning, collaborative working, information flows, opportunity spotting, audit, open book accounting and benefits management.

The ability to cope with change is a key factor. It is impossible to construct an infinitely flexible deal, but you can identify principles, processes and behaviours that set out how you and your provider plan to deal with change.

If you already have a draft contract, it will form the basis for the actual contract between you and your provider. The content of an Output Based Specification may also become part of the contract. The standard terms and conditions can be drawn from previously created model agreements (see below), or there may be terms and conditions that your organisation has already decided upon. The requirements for the particular acquisition are then added to these terms to form the schedules for the contract, which detail the specific services in the contract and how they are to be delivered.

OGC Model Agreements

OGC Model Agreements are a selection of specifically designed model contracts. Developed for the public sector over eight years and representing acknowledged best practice, they are now used by both the public and private sector alike. The Model Agreements are regularly updated to align with all EC and UK legislative changes and to incorporate new legal thinking and government policy changes.

A CD-ROM of OGC Model Agreements is published by TSO, containing a portfolio of model contracts including system supply, system support, services, commodities and frameworks. They are designed to act as a starting point for contract drafting, and to be customised to suit individual needs and circumstances. It is recommended, however, that such customisation be undertaken with the help of procurement experts and legal advisors.

Unforeseen changes

A key issue in constructing far-reaching or complex agreements is the ability of the contract to withstand change. Contracts may address this need for flexibility in various ways, including:

- **service flexibilities:** ensuring that contractual provisions allow for ways in which contracted services may vary with time; for example, by providing expressly for fluctuations in volume or service performance to reflect potential changes in business need

- **technology refreshment provisions:** where the provider bears responsibility and risk for the continuing effectiveness of the technical infrastructure, there is a need to specify how technology refreshment will be managed

- **costed options:** many contracts define optional services, which the customer can take up at any stage. An obvious difficulty is balancing the effort of defining, in adequate contractual terms, services that may never be taken up, while a significant advantage is knowing the cost of taking up any such option

- **including terms and conditions** that explicitly provide for dealing with issues such as legislative change, or other issues which impose obligations of flexibility on the provider (or on the customer)

- **providing for access to resources or facilities** in the wider provider organisation, beyond the core scope of the contract, to enable the customer to acquire information or resources that meet new or short-term needs.

In practice, a balance has to be struck between three requirements: flexibility, affordability and value for money over time.

Other issues to consider before contract award

Other areas that need to be thought through before the contract is signed include:

- how will you achieve the level of control you need?

- do you understand the technical direction in which the provider is taking your organisation? You must be able to have a dialogue with the provider and understand the implications for your business in their answers

- how would the provider ensure that they could always provide you with sufficient skilled resources, given the problems of national skills shortages and the risk that another customer's account might take priority?

- what is the real quality of the provider team? Do they have sufficient standing within their organisation to ensure that they will be able to get the resources you require? Can they influence their own board?

- is there a likelihood of a loss of continuity with the provider team changing after award of contract?

- if the provider is a consortium, how will the members handle things and ensure that problems are resolved quickly and constructively? For example, do all members of the consortium share the same quality management system and/or escalation procedures?

- what does the provider know about your business and current IT operation and how will they get up to speed? Can you ensure that enough time is allowed for the provider's learning curve in understanding the complexity of your business?

Foundations for contract management

During the procurement process, your focus is likely to be on why the contract is being established and on whether the provider will be able to deliver. However, you must also think very carefully about how the contract will work once it has been awarded.

Management of contracts, especially where there is a partnership, requires flexibility on both sides and a willingness to adapt the terms of the contract to reflect a rapidly changing world.

As the customer, you must have clear business objectives and a clear understanding of how the contract will contribute to them. You must be able to recognise and get agreed at senior management level the need for the provider to achieve their objectives, including making a reasonable margin, perhaps as part of a risk/reward arrangement. Make sure that you understand, and do not neglect, the provider's objectives; they will be less willing to be flexible if you regard them as 'just a provider'.

There must be people with the right interpersonal and management skills to manage relationships on a peer-to-peer basis and at multiple levels in the organisation. Both sides need managers who can manage upwards in their organisation and persuade their boards to make decisions for the benefit of the joint relationship (even when individual decisions may not look attractive in themselves).

Contract checklist

This checklist sets out the principal aspects that should be considered before the contract is finalised:

- the optimum pricing and performance mechanism (fixed price or varying with usage, for example)

- other key commercial features such as profit caps, benefit-based payments, price/performance model, duration extensions and duration reductions (early termination)

- duration of the contract

- intellectual property rights (IPR) ownership

- legacy systems/data migration

- alternative revenue/spare capacity usage

- incentives to improve performance

- plan and method for implementation and testing

- ability to respond as the organisation changes, limiting or sharing the cost of change

- the risks associated with a particular business model, which may include:

  - lock-in

  - guaranteeing continuing value for money

  - benefits achievement

  - risks that either the organisation or the provider cannot manage change

  - loss of business continuity when staff are transferred

  - risk allocation

- the organisation's behaviour – what behaviour do we need to exhibit to make the business model work?

  - responsiveness

  - openness, including commercial information

  - readiness for innovation/willingness to work in new ways, including the acceptance of risk

  - collaborative approach/attitude

  - seeking benefit versus cost-consciousness

- providers' behaviour – what behaviour does the provider need to exhibit to make the business model work?

- proactivity

- sharing ideas and commercial information

- readiness to explore/discuss problems

- working collaboratively with the organisation and/or other providers

- take-up of options

- exit strategies/strategies for termination and recompetition

- the organisation's skills:

  - technical and general skills

  - ability to manage change

  - strategy setting

  - understanding of the business

  - business requirement elicitation and assurance

  - knowledge transfer from procurement team to contract manager (or contract management team)

- providers' skills:

  - technical and general skills

  - ability to manage change

  - technology exploitation

  - process re-engineering.

6.6 Provider debriefing	If the requirement was advertised in the OJEC, the successful provider must also be announced there. It is also good practice, and obligatory if providers request it, to debrief all tenderers on the reasons for their success or failure.
	It is important to let providers know your reasons for rejecting them, since silence may lead them to the conclusion that price was the only factor. Ensure that your emphasis on value for money follows through into the debriefing stage, so that providers understand all the factors that had a bearing on your decision.
6.7 Decision point: investment decision	This decision point focuses on final checks before the contract is awarded and an investment is made in a service.
	Now that bid information has been evaluated and confirmed, you should confirm that it will meet the requirements of the business case and deliver the intended benefits. The chosen provider and contract must be able to deliver the specified

outputs or outcomes on time and within budget. The service contract should also represent value for money for the customer organisation.

You should check that all statutory and procedural requirements have been followed during the acquisition process.

Contract management issues, including lines of communication, governance, flexibility and plans for recompetition should also be examined before investment is made. Where appropriate, these issues should be explored with the provider rather than in isolation.

This decision point corresponds with OGC Gateway Review 3 (see Annex E).

Implementation

7

This chapter deals with implementation: bringing the service on-stream and preparing for this event.

Implementation is hard work, and is often considered to be the most difficult task of strategic management. If a major new service is to be implemented, with IT components, there must be rigorous management of the change. There must also be adequate resources. Recent research shows that preparing the organisation for the change can consume 80% of the resources for a project (through requirements for training, development of new processes etc), with the IT spend accounting for only 20%.

Implementation of a new service should take place in accordance with a programme or project plan; ideally this plan would already be part of the contract. It may mean a major change for the organisation and therefore requires careful planning and adequate resources. This chapter outlines what needs to be considered for successful implementation and transition to an operational service.

Implementation of a new service involves three areas of activity:

- development (where there are new systems and processes)
- transition
- operational services.

Development

Development activities ensure that the organisation and providers are prepared; they take place before the new service goes 'live'. New ways of working may require rethinking of policies, procedures and service delivery arrangements, followed by the testing of pilot versions of new systems and processes. IT applications may need to be developed as part of the service contract, or acquired at the same time, perhaps through a third party or developed in-house. Staff need to be involved closely through the development stage, participating in the design and planning of new ways of working and receiving training as required. Adequate communication with staff is a critical factor for success in managing the change.

Transition

Transition involves the introduction of the new arrangements into the organisation and the roll-out of new or changed IT facilities. Two approaches could be taken:

- 'big bang', in which the transition is made in one step

- incremental change, in which the new arrangements are gradually introduced one step at a time.

The transition stage should be planned as a distinct state, different from both the current and future states. It may be necessary to implement interim arrangements for the transition period, perhaps with the old and new ways of working running in parallel until everything has been tested in a live working environment. The transition period is likely to be a period of stress and uncertainty; planning for the transition must take account of the concerns of those inside and outside the organisation who will be affected or need to be kept informed. Where there is major change, transition is often planned and structured as a project. It would be advisable to address the issue of transition and its management as part of the contract.

Operational services

Following a successful transition, the new arrangements become operational. Organisational change may involve changes in the relationships within the organisation and with external providers, perhaps with a number of new service providers working together in partnership with other public sector organisations to deliver shared services to the public. Effective mechanisms must be in place for benefits realisation, service management, performance monitoring and contract management.

All of the implementation activities will take place within the Programme Management framework established for the change effort, as described in detail in OGC's *Managing Successful Programmes* guidance.

7.1 Readiness for a new service

When a new service is about to be delivered, several groups need to be ready for the change and supporting activities must be in place. For example, Organisation X is planning to implement electronic services to the public, with a single point of contact to a call centre and a website providing information for the public (see section 4.1 outlining Organisation X's desired outcomes). The checklist below summarises what needs to be done.

Successful implementation requires that:

- the organisation is ready

  - processes have been thoroughly worked out, tested and are ready to go 'live'

  - information and support is available (for example, customer information and scripts are ready at a call centre, with access to skilled resources as required)

  - responsibilities are identified and in place (clearly defining who is going to do what, as outlined further down in this checklist)

  - contract management is in place

  - the contract management team has worked through the detail of administering the contract and is familiar with its aims and purpose

- staff are ready

  - they know what is expected of them

  - training has been given at the right time

- the public are ready

  - they are aware and can find out more if they want

- providers are ready

  - they know what is expected of them

  - systems have been tested and are ready for roll-out

  - contract management is in place

  - the contract management team has worked through the detail of administering the contract and is familiar with its aims and purpose

- service management is in place

  - details of the service level agreements have been worked through and agreed by both parties

- benefits management is in place

  - a benefits management regime has been set up, with nominated individuals responsible for ensuring that benefits will be achieved

- performance measurement is in place

  - the current performance is baselined

  - measures are identified and agreed

  - responsibilities of both/all parties are clearly understood

- changes ahead have been considered

- flexibility is built into the contract as required.

Detailed guidance on the organisation's readiness for change is provided in the companion volume *How to manage Business Change*; detailed guidance on managing operational services and their performance is found in the companion volumes *How to manage Service Provision* and *How to manage Performance*.

7.2 **Contingency plans**   Your organisation must ensure that it has plans in place to ensure business continuity in the event of the provider failing to deliver. This contingency plan should be tested rigorously with service providers and regularly updated as part of your organisation's business continuity planning.

You may decide that complete, 100% cover for the service is not justifiable in terms of cost, in which case you have to decide what reduced level of service would be acceptable, and for how long it would be acceptable for the service to run at this level. Another way to view this is in terms of the risk to your business while you are without the service. Define the acceptable level of risk, in terms of the service being unavailable, and make plans so that risk never exceeds that level.

Contingency plans might also have to be devised for the possibility that take-up of the service is not as good as was hoped, particularly if it is a service provided direct to the public. However, your choice of a business model (section 3.3) should have involved consideration of how the new service will be promoted and how take-up will be encouraged.

For more information on managing risk, consult the OGC *Guidelines on Managing Risk*.

7.3 **Decision point: readiness for service**   This decision point focuses on ensuring that both customer and provider are prepared for the new service to begin operation.

You should ensure that the contractual arrangements are up to date and that, if applicable, the provider has fulfilled the relevant parts of it on time. Check that the business case is still valid, that it has not been affected by internal or external changes or events since the acquisition began, and that the service is still on course to deliver the business benefit that was intended at that point.

All necessary testing, including issues such as business integration and user acceptance, should be completed to the customer's satisfaction, and there should be feasible and tested contingency plans. All ongoing risks should still be under effective management so that they will not threaten the implementation process.

Finally, you should check that any lessons learned from this acquisition will be recorded so that the organisation is able to improve.

This decision point corresponds with OGC Gateway Review 4 (see Annex E).

Making it work

8

This chapter briefly covers some of the issues that you will need to address after contract award. Your main concern will be keeping everything running smoothly, dealing with any problems that come up and ensuring that you and your provider are happy with the arrangement and getting the benefits for which you both hoped.

There is more detail on this topic in the companion guide *How to manage Service Provision*, which deals with the management of contracts after they have been awarded. However, this chapter will also be useful as an indicator of what will be required later; it is worth reading even at early stages of the procurement or partnership process.

8.1 Managing the contract

Contract management is the process that ensures parties in a contract meet their obligations, to deliver the required objectives and give value for money. Typically, you will require resources for contract management that are equivalent to 2% of the contract value. It is an integral part of the 'intelligent customer' role.

Critical success factors

A contract is being managed successfully if the following conditions are met:

- the arrangements for service delivery continue to be satisfactory to both customer and provider

- the expected business benefits and value for money are being realised

- the provider is co-operative and responsive

- the customer knows their obligations under the contract

- changes are being dealt with to mutual satisfaction

- disputes are dealt with effectively and to mutual agreement

- there are no surprises.

Contract communication

A common complaint following contract award relates to inconsistent communication between customer and provider organisations. Senior managers of both parties are often seen to be positive and forward thinking; working level links between technical staff or with users are also good. Problems are most often reported at a middle-management level where contract and account managers are measured on short-term financial performance. At this level, the contract and enforcing its provisions may tend to dominate the relationship. To help prevent this, the contract should establish clear lines of communication at all levels in both organisations, and define procedures for escalating difficult problems to higher management levels.

Managing changes to the contract

Inevitably, there will be changes to manage over the lifetime of the contract. Costs and disruption to the business will be much reduced if flexibility has been built into the contract from the outset.

Flexibility in a contract can be divided into two types:

- flexibility in terms of options in the contract (contractual flexibility) for issues that can be foreseen at the time of the contract award (see section 6.5)

- flexibility in terms of a framework (within the contract or extra-contractually) that will encourage flexibility in the relationship for issues that have not been foreseen.

Measuring performance

You will usually need performance measures to cover all aspects of a service arrangement:

- cost and value obtained

- performance and customer satisfaction

- delivery improvement and added value

- delivery capability

- benefits realised

- relationship strength and responsiveness.

Ideally, performance measures are specified in the contract.

Once chosen, the requirements underpinning the performance measures should be the primary focus for contract management. They should provide the framework around which provider information requirements and flows, contract management teams, skills, processes and activities are developed.

It is important that the performance measures selected offer clear and demonstrable evidence of the success of the relationship. You should have an existing baseline against which to track improvements. This baseline will typically be established in the business case for the deal.

There is more detailed guidance on this topic in the companion guide *How to manage Performance*.

8.2 Managing the relationship

Relationship management means ensuring that both parties can work together. It involves setting up effective reporting arrangements and building the attitudes and behaviours that encourage mutual success.

Why is it important?

Major service contracts typically involve a high degree of dependence and commitment, for whatever period, between the parties. From your perspective, you are committed to a certain provider or providers. The provider in turn is committed to providing resources to meet your requirements. The costs involved in changing provider mid-term are likely to be high and the contract may make it highly unattractive – although the requirement to recompete means that public sector organisations need always to consider such a possibility.

In addition to the contractual and commercial aspects of the contract already discussed, the relationship between the parties – the way they regard each other and the way in which the arrangement operates – is crucial to making a success of the contract.

The ability to accommodate change successfully is fundamental to the success of any commercial relationship that is to succeed over time. In particular, you need to be able to respond to changes in what you require from the relationship. A constructive approach to managing the relationship will make change much easier to work through.

Critical success factors

When deciding how you will manage the relationship, the following points are crucial:

- the relationship needs to be championed at senior levels in both organisations (or each organisation, where there are multiple partners)

- always remember that the attitudes and actions demonstrated by senior management will lead the tone of the relationship

- governance arrangements must be equitable and relationships must be peer-to-peer. If not, imbalances will occur

- a large number of formal management levels should be avoided, but some differentiation is required to ensure that long-term strategic issues are considered as well as day-to-day service delivery aspects. These are best separated to avoid urgent and pressing matters constantly swamping the longer view

- formal committee structures should not be seen as overly rigid

- roles and responsibilities should be clear and staff involved in managing the relationship need to be suitably empowered

- escalation and dispute resolution routes should be understood and used properly – encourage an approach that seeks to resolve problems early, without escalating up the management chain (or to third parties) unnecessarily.

Principles of good communication

You have to be aware of new demands when working together – who takes the lead, who is responsible for what, who pays for what. Will your existing management structures help or hinder the new arrangement? You may require different reporting arrangements, depending on your organisational structure, but the underlying principles of good communication and mutual understanding of responsibilities remain the same.

There must be a clear understanding of what is expected and effective ways of reporting progress. You must have a formal framework defining responsibilities, reporting arrangements and policies. Without this framework there is a risk that you will lose control; your auditors will also need to be assured that formal arrangements are in place, whether you operate a 'hands-on' or 'hands-off' management style.

8.3 Decision point: benefits evaluation

This final decision point concerns the evaluation of the benefits resulting from the service being in full operation.

The primary concern is to ensure that all the benefits that were hoped for are actually being delivered. This may also involve the production of a Full Business Case, which adds in actual real-world information gained from the experience of the acquisition. It also confirms that the previous business case was sound and that it correctly identified a business need that is now being met.

The contract should still be meeting a business need. If circumstances or requirements have changed, the delivery of the service and the contract that describes it should be changing. If there is divergence, urgent action should be taken to rectify this.

The arrangements for managing the contract – and the relationship – should be re-examined to ensure that they are still adequate and ideally that they will deliver improvements in value for money over the life of the contract. There should be plans and sufficient resource to continue managing the contract to its conclusion, as well as a viable exit strategy and arrangements for recompetition.

This decision point corresponds with OGC Gateway Review 5 (see Annex E).

Recompetition

9

Recompetition is what happens at the end of a contract – the exit strategy from the old contract and the process of creating a new one. The larger the contract, the more attention needs to be paid to recompetition.

This chapter explores the options at the end of a contract. It seeks to provide a framework for the decision-making processes surrounding recompetition and to highlight the issues to be addressed in ensuring a successful handover.

9.1 The benefits of recompetition

For the customer, the process of recompetition can be desirable because:

- it provides an opportunity to gain leverage, extracting better value and service than might otherwise have been obtained

- it provides an incentive for providers to become more innovative in their solutions to the challenges faced by the customer. New offerings in the market can be given a chance to compete, and the incumbent will need to produce more imaginative solutions to the challenges faced to stand a chance of winning

- it allows for greater flexibility, necessary to comply with the customer organisation's strategic needs. The contract can be re-scoped to accommodate changes in the business plan

- it forces the customer to re-evaluate needs, subject to the rigorous preparation of a new business case. Without recompetition and with many other pressures on management time, there may otherwise be a temptation simply to extend the contract on similar terms, on the basis that it has worked well so far. Preparing the business case for the recompetition may result in a fresh appraisal of needs, leading to a solution more in accordance with the business strategy.

A carefully considered exit strategy is also important in helping to reduce the potentially overwhelming advantage of the incumbent provider. There should 7be a clearly prepared exit strategy from the outset of the relationship, not just at recompetition. It should be seen as a confidence builder, providing a reassuring safety net for both parties, not as 'planning for disaster'.

Recompetition is both necessary and desirable. Organisations must face up to it early and not underestimate the challenges involved in both successfully planning and implementing the search for the new provider and managing the handover.

9.2 Reassessing business need

Recompetition starts with a return to the business need that gave rise to the acquisition of the service in the first place. Other issues, such as what kind of arrangement is appropriate for the new procurement and the scope of the new contract, should 'cascade' from business need.

The first step is to establish what, if any, needs there actually will be for the foreseeable future. The high-level drivers need to be considered, so that the nature of the business needs both now and in the future can be evaluated.

This means considering questions such as:

- does the old contract still meet business need?

- if a new arrangement on similar lines is created, will it meet needs in the future as well as now?

- which of the services delivered under the old contract are still required?

- are there new requirements?

- how could the new requirements be met?

- what initiatives (government-wide and departmental) will impact on this recompetition?

- what kind of arrangement is appropriate now?

- has sufficient expertise been retained to be sure of running a successful re-procurement?

Figure 4 (overleaf) outlines the process of recompetition. The steps followed and the questions asked will mirror the original procurement in many ways, but will now take account of developments in business needs, policy demands, market developments and the lessons learned from the contract.

Other organisations

Other public sector organisations should also be considered:

- what business requirements does the organisation have in common with others in the public sector that can be jointly sourced, or which can be provided through another's sourcing arrangements?

- has another organisation set up a framework agreement for commodity services that could be used?

- do the terms of the existing framework allow for the addition of new customers?

Look at the experiences of others in the public sector to identify opportunities for improvement. There needs to be a greater appreciation of the importance of a

Figure 4
Planning the recompetition

A flowchart showing the questions that should be asked and the options at each stage. Note the identification of needs that precedes any consideration of the contract arrangements

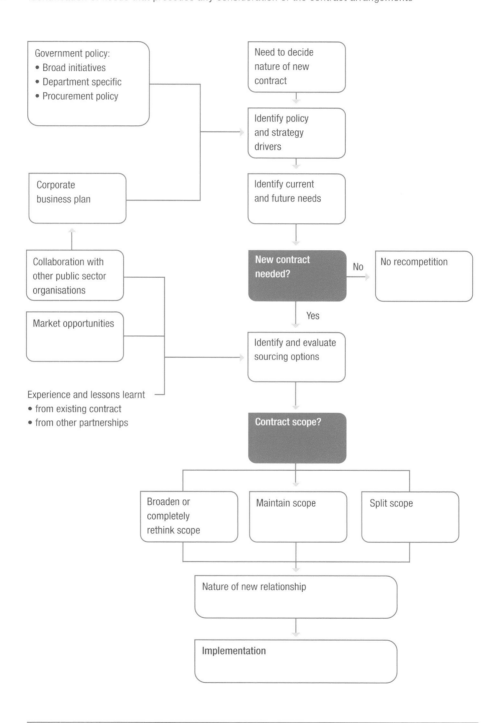

well-planned exit strategy, which reduces the hold of the incumbent and smoothes the transition. This includes providing financial incentives for the provider to perform well right up to the end of the contract.

9.3 Looking at sourcing options

As with the initial acquisition, once business need has been identified, the options for sourcing need to be examined. The issues to consider are:

- how best to provide currently outsourced services for which there will be a future need

- how best to provide services currently supplied in-house, for which there will be a future need

- how best to provide services for which there will be only a limited future need

- how best to provide totally new services or capture new means of providing existing services.

Consider first the existing relationship. In deciding what form a future outsourcing might take, there is clearly much to learn from the current relationship. What scope is there for improvement? This can take the form of a systematic evaluation of different aspects of the relationship, either internally or with the advice of external consultancy.

Factors to consider include:

- range of services

- flexibility of contract

- customer's reaction and adjustment to outsourcing

- exit strategy

- 'informed partner' capabilities

- quality and focus of service: did the provider deliver services to a high quality and on time? Were the provider's incentives structured to ensure buy-in to the customer's objectives?

Scoping scenarios

The key decision to be addressed is the scope of the new contract or contracts. The options are:

- to retain the scope of the existing contract

- to split the scope of the existing contract

- to broaden the scope of the existing contract, perhaps to expand it into a strategic alliance or partnership

- to completely rethink the requirement for the contract.

Cascading from this scoping decision will be the nature of the new contract or contracts; what kind of relationship is required with a provider, including its length and funding arrangements?

Note that bringing services back in-house once they have been contracted out is not listed as an option. This is an extreme measure, often not viable (particularly if the decision to outsource was properly thought through); the skills will not be available in-house to make it possible.

The decision will, of course, be dependent upon the individual circumstances of the organisation. However, many organisations will face similar issues. The first thing to do is to look at the key options that involve changing the scope. These are summarised in table 1.

Table 1 Options for broadening or splitting the scope of a procurement	Broaden scope	Split scope
	Combine service under single provider	Split services to multiple providers
	Add value added services, such as Business Process Re-engineering	
	Add high-risk tailored services	Separate out services for commodity provision
	Perhaps through joint procurement	*Perhaps through joint procurement*

Broadening the scope may be a matter of taking functions currently managed by different providers and bundling them into one package. Conversely, the recompetition may be used as an opportunity to widen the range of providers or split services off for commodity provision.

One provider or more?   The decision on single or multiple providers is not straightforward; the number of providers must be decided on a case-by-case basis. A possible compromise is the prime contractor approach (see section 5.1), where one provider is given overall responsibility for managing sub-providers. This does not give the customer the same level of control over the sub-providers and can lengthen the supply chain, but otherwise captures many advantages of both solutions.

If there are already several interdependent contracts making up the service, the issues to be considered will include:

- what is the effect on the overall service of replacing one component of it?

- should the entire service be re-constituted on a different basis?

- if so, how should the ends of the component contracts be synchronised?

What kind of contract?

There is a broad trend towards relationships becoming more sophisticated, extending towards higher value-added processes such as control of business functions. This represents a major re-evaluation of the relationship between customers and providers. Concurrent with this change in scope must be a deepening of the relationship.

If it is decided that a new contract along similar lines to the old one is in the best interests of the organisation, then special care must be taken in managing the recompetition. How will an open and fair recompetition be ensured? How will other potential providers be encouraged to bid? In the absence of substantial competition, how will the best possible value for money deal be obtained? If there is a change in provider, then all the implementation challenges associated with other recompetitions still apply.

Careful planning and management of the handover from incumbent to new provider(s) is of crucial importance to ensuring business continuity.

9.4 The handover

The handover process is driven by the need to ensure business continuity during a period of major upheaval. This is especially important if the handover is mid-project. In addition, public sector organisations have an obligation in law, and as a matter of public policy, to do what they can to create the environment for an effective and open competitive environment (the 'level playing field'). Whether this is an easy task or not will depend on a number of factors.

The key issues that need to be addressed when a commercial agreement is approaching its conclusion are:

- investment towards the end of the relationship

- people issues

- the end-to-end lead time that will be required to get a new provider up and running

- handover obligations on the potentially outgoing provider

- physical assets (that is, IT equipment and other tangible property)

- software

- data.

In considering the handover, special attention should be given to the assurance of business continuity and how to ensure a genuine competition in the presence of a potential advantage to the incumbent. Begin planning the exit strategy early, at the procurement stage, and include a transfer of responsibility agreement. Consider incentives for a successful handover, such as retention of funds or asset inspection – see HM Treasury guidance on Standardisation of PFI Contracts (IT) for more detailed advice.

Finally, there are occasional circumstances where a delay to the recompetition is desirable on business grounds. Properly handled, this could be in the long-term interests of effective competition.

Roles and responsibilities

10

The roles involved in acquisition of major services are senior management, the business manager (or managers) responsible for the requirement, the procurement team (or an equivalent team where there is already a provider in place) and a range of advisers, whose expertise will vary depending on the acquisition.

For simplicity, it is assumed that only one organisation is involved in the acquisition; in practice (especially in government) there may be several organisations working together. In such situations there must be one senior manager with overall responsibility for a successful outcome (the Senior Responsible Owner or Project Owner); there may be several procurement teams working in parallel who will need to co-ordinate their activities. There may also be a team of external advisers appointed to develop the requirement before inviting bids from potential providers; this scenario is discussed below.

10.1 Senior management

The principal role is that of the Senior Responsible Owner/Project Owner, or equivalent senior role responsible for the overall success of the business change and services to which the acquisition contributes.

The organisation's management board is responsible for ensuring that value for money is achieved from the procurement. It is their role to make a business judgement (with expert advice where required) if providers' solutions and prices differ widely. Their task is to determine whether additional benefits are worth paying for, compared with similar offerings that deliver fewer business benefits and a lower price.

10.2 Business managers

The business managers whose requirements will be met by the procurement are responsible for:

- identifying the business requirement

- overseeing interpretation of the business requirement into service specifications

- setting performance targets at the level of business outcome.

As part of the task of identifying the requirement, business managers are responsible for ensuring that the needs of end-users will be met. This may not be within the organisation's direct control – for example, there may need to be consultation with members of the public or their representatives as potential end users.

10.3 The procurement team

The procurement team roles must include:

- a project manager leading the procurement project

- a team member taking the lead on commercial and procurement issues, with strong negotiating skills and access to additional support if required (for example, legal support)

- a team member taking the lead on service operational and technical assurance

- support from team members with detailed knowledge of the business and financial modelling skills for developing the business case.

The range of skills required is outlined below.

When developing a procurement strategy, team members will need skills in:

- scoping possible deals

- identifying sourcing options, including existing arrangements

- seeking opportunities for collaboration with other organisations as required – including learning from their earlier experiences

- identifying constraints; 'sounding out' the services marketplace

- addressing contract management considerations

When identifying and specifying requirements, skills will be needed in:

- analysis of requirements for services; assessing alternative opportunities for service delivery; determining feasibility

- co-ordinating business/user input to requirements analysis and specification, with other organisations and user communities as appropriate

- developing and advising on business cases; business case authorisation or rejection

- producing appropriate documents to specify requirements for services, feeding into the procurement process (such as prospectuses, output based specifications)

- ensuring compliance with existing policies and programme plans

During the procurement process, when managing deals/procurements, skills will be needed in:

- identifying the optimum balance of risk and reward in potential deals

- (for public sector procurements) deciding appropriate procurement routes; identifying and advertising future procurement requirements

- (for public sector procurements) managing the procurement process in accordance with EC legislation, government and organisation policies;

- evaluating proposals against agreed criteria

- negotiating deals and contract terms.

When planning and managing implementation of a new service, skills will be needed in:

- managing transition to new services, systems and providers

- gaining the user community's acceptance, whether they are internal staff or members of the public.

10.4 Professional advisers

Advisers will be needed throughout the procurement process. They may be part of the organisation's own staff, but are often brought in from external sources for the duration of the project. For large-scale construction projects, for example, there may be a preliminary procurement to acquire a project team to develop the requirement; for PFI projects there may be appointment of commercial specialists to advise on the scope of the proposed deal.

Some advisers, such as procurement experts, will be required early on in the process and will continue to contribute throughout; others will be required at specific stages. The range of expertise required will vary from project to project, but will always include advisers on procurement processes, legal advisers and technical experts (which includes expertise in construction, property and IT-related issues). For PFI procurements, it is essential to seek expert financial advice – if not available in-house then usually from merchant and investment banks and major accountancy firms. Some experts may be retained throughout the life of the contract, such as advisers on the conduct of contract management.

Expert advisers are an expensive resource. To make the most of them, you should ensure that:

- credentials of advisers are checked and their knowledge, commitment and depth of resource are tested

- the role of advisers is made clear to all involved in working with them. It is important to note that advisers cannot take decisions on behalf of the customer; it remains the department's responsibility to decide on issues such as contract schedules, basing their decisions on the advice of experts

- they are all properly managed, and remain focused only on their particular assigned role or task.

In the public sector, it is essential that advisers are selected through competition. You should take care to ensure that your organisation's ability to award a contract by competition is not prejudiced by any earlier involvement of an adviser.

For more information about sources of advice on the appointment of advisers, see the further information section at the end of this document.

Annexes

Model of an output based specification

An output based specification (OBS) focuses on the desired outputs of a service in business terms, rather than a detailed technical specification of how the service is to be provided; this allows providers scope to propose innovative solutions that might not have occurred to the procurement team.

This listing suggests a framework for the contents of an OBS for a business service based procurement. It is not intended that this framework should be prescriptive; the OBS for any procurement should reflect the requirements of the customer organisation and the circumstances of the procurement. The headings and contents lists will need to be tailored for each procurement situation.

Introduction

Section headings to include:

- introduction to customer organisation

- introduction to OBS: purpose, composition

- disclaimers, caveats etc

- confidentiality, IPR.

Background to the requirement

Section headings to include:

- organisational business – overview

- business strategy

- current functions and structure relevant to procurement

- current IS/IT relevant to procurement

- policies, standards

- history relevant to procurement – recent developments

- future developments relevant to procurement

- objectives of PFI for procurement (where relevant)

- role of this procurement in business plans

- scope of this procurement – summary:

  - core service provision (basic and business-specific)

  - core service provision – business services

  - optional extensions for which proposals will be considered

  - services, business activities excluded from procurement.

Specification of requirements

Section headings to include:

- description of business area affected by procurement
- business environment: related activities, stakeholders
- overview of business objectives relevant to procurement
- description of the business activities in the area affected by procurement:
  - business functions and processes
  - organisation and staffing: roles and responsibilities
  - information flows
  - current service support
  - quantitative aspects of current operations
- scope of procurement (initial view)
- basic/infrastructure services to be provided
- business-specific services to be provided
- business services to be provided
- other services required (eg. training)
- specification of services, products and states/conditions desired
- requirements to be met – essential outputs, measures, quality attributes, performance
- possibilities, options for variation in scope of procurement:
  - extension to encompass additional business activities within specified business functions
  - extension of scope of support for specified business activities
  - extension of scope to include support for other business functions
- future developments required, options
- constraints on solutions (minimum set), eg:
  - compatibility
  - interfacing, interworking
  - standards
  - interaction with other business activities
- requirements/constraints for migration, implementation, cut-over, start-up

- requirements for additional services, eg. further development, consultancy
- scope for transfer of assets, staff
- risks to be considered by providers.

Contract and service management requirements

Sections to include:

- expected nature of contracts; proposed terms and conditions
- opportunities for suggesting different contract scopes
- proposed arrangements for management of contract
- requirements/constraints for service management, customer liaison
- roles and responsibilities.

Procurement procedures

Sections to include:

- procurement timetable
- implementation timetable - requirements
- procurement procedures
- information required on costs
- evaluation criteria, procedures.

Response required to OBS

Sections to include information required, such as:

- corporate capability
    - such as nature of consortium
- response to service requirements
    - service provision
    - business service provision
    - other services offered
- description of approach to service provision (method statement)
    - specific topics to be addressed (checklist)
    - project management and implementation
    - plans and timetable
    - organisation and staffing

- commercial proposals (indicative/budgetary); response of provider:

  - funding arrangements

  - basis of charging

  - budgetary costs

  - incentives in contract: provider's proposals

  - transfer of assets, staff

  - other revenue streams

- response to contract requirements

- management of risk; risk transfer: response of provider

- options, alternative proposals.

Format for responses

- details of layout required for ease of comparison, evaluation.

Annexes

- details not included in main document, eg:

  - details of business activities

  - business facts and figures

  - organisational details

  - details of current services, technical environment

  - requirements for compatibility, interfacing.

Business case template

The information set out below should be used as a starting point for developing your own business cases. The information content is presented here for convenience as five key aspects of the business case: strategic fit, options appraisal, achievability, affordability and commercial aspects. You should tailor this structure as required for your project. Note that the commercial aspects of the business case will only apply where there is an external procurement relating to the project; however, organisations using partnerships or framework arrangements will also find these principles useful.

The business case is developed in three stages:

- preliminary business case (or Strategic Outline Case) to confirm strategic fit and business need

- Outline Business Case – indicative assumptions to support the preferred way forward (including procurement strategy, where applicable)

- Full Business Case – validated assumptions to support the investment decision.

The level of detail required at each stage depends on your organisational standards and the scale or complexity of your project.

1 Strategic fit

This aspect of the business case explains how the scope of the proposed project fits within the existing business and IS/IT strategies of the organisation; and the compelling case for change, in terms of the existing and future operational needs of the organisation.

Minimum content needed for this section: description of the organisation's key business objectives, the business need and its contribution to the organisation's business strategy, key benefits to be realised.

Areas that could be considered in detail are outlined below.

1.1 Organisational overview

Describe the organisation's main aims, organisational structure and key responsibilities

1.2 Business strategy and themes

Describe the strategic vision, strategic plan and continuing aims

1.3 IS/IT strategy and objectives (where IT-related business change is a key aspect)	Outline the IS/IT strategic themes in your business/IS strategy (such as delivering information electronically to the public, enabling transactions electronically), key programmes and projects
1.4 Investment objectives	Set out the case for change in terms of investment objectives such as 'to improve the quality of the organisation's business services through the integrated, improved and expanded use of IS/IT'; 'to future-proof the organisation in terms of its ability to deliver agreed work programmes in accordance with legislative changes and wider government policies'
1.5 Existing arrangements	Outline the current technological environment (e.g. IT infrastructure), service delivery arrangements, major contracts with service providers, the in-house function, where applicable
1.6 Business need and service gaps	This sub-section links to the investment objectives above. Identify business needs and service gaps in relation to major government initiatives such as Achieving Excellence and the Modernising Government agenda, the organisation's business programmes and its operational requirements
1.7 Scope: minimum, desirable and optional	Summarise the potential scope of requirement against a continuum of need, ranging from a minimum or core scope (replacement of existing services) to a desirable scope (core plus some other contracts and business improvement) to an optional scope. Suggested number of options: up to seven at a high level, to ensure that the scope has been thoroughly explored
1.8 Constraints	Summarise the main constraints, such as the willingness of senior management to absorb fundamental business change, the affordability of proposals, existing contractual commitments
1.9 Dependencies	Outline the internal and external factors upon which the successful delivery of this project are dependent, such as other projects and programmes already underway
1.10 Strategic benefits	Outline high-level strategic and operational benefits such as minimised development costs, maximised use of corporate information
1.11 Strategic risks	Outline business risks such as continuing need for the service and changes in business direction; service risks such as the lack of internal skills to implement the required projects; external environmental risks such as availability of PFI funding

2 Options appraisal

This aspect of the business case, in accordance with HM Treasury's Green Book, documents the wide range of options which have been considered within the broad scope identified in response to the organisation's existing and future business needs.

Minimum content needed for this section: high-level cost/benefit analysis of at least three options for meeting the business need; include analysis of 'soft' benefits that cannot be quantified in financial terms; identify preferred option.

Areas that could be considered in detail are outlined below.

2.1 Long and short list of options

Outline options identified for analysis (described more fully below), where appropriate each subjected to SWOT analysis against investment objectives and critical success factors includes a 'do minimum' option and at least two but no more than seven other options.

2.2 Critical success factors

Explore critical success factors of business needs, strategic fit, benefits optimisation, risk management and potential achievability, provider capacity and capability, potential affordability

2.3 Scoping options

Outline up to seven scoping options from 'do nothing' to major business improvement, with brief description of each, advantages/disadvantages and conclusions

2.4 Solution sets

Consider the range of potential technology which could be used to support the services required by the organisation within the parameters of the desired scope for the project; the detail will be determined during the course of procurement or detailed study with existing providers

2.5 Service delivery options

Investigate options ranging from in-house delivery to degrees of partnership with the private sector and with others in the public sector: with brief description of each, advantages/disadvantages and conclusions

2.6 Implementation options

For Outline Business Case: examine options for the pace at which the contracted services could be implemented, in terms of the timescales and degree of business change required; investigate shortlisted options of 'do minimum', public sector comparator (for PFI projects), more ambitious and less ambitious options

2.7 Detailed options appraisal

Provide an explanation of the general approach taken to the calculation of costs and benefits, together with overview of the key findings that result from each of the shortlisted options. To include details of 'soft' benefits, that is, benefits that do not have a direct financial value.

2.8 Risk quantification and sensitivity analysis	For risk quantification show the 'cost of risk retained' under each option: risk category (e.g. legislative risks); related key risks (e.g. changes in primary legislation leading to cost increases); where appropriate (e.g. for PFI) include value in £ sterling. Supplement this information by the organisation's high-level risk register.

For sensitivity analysis show the effect of changes in crucial factors to each option, for PFI projects this should be expressed as percentage increase or decrease from the public sector comparator. |
| *2.9 Benefits appraisal* | Show results of identifying key benefits criteria, weighting their relative importance, scoring shortlisted options against those criteria; where required derive a weighted benefits score for each option and undertake an analysis of the sensitivity of the assessment to changes in weighting and scoring. |
| *2.10 Preferred option* | Summarise findings from economic appraisals, benefits evaluation, sensitivity analysis and overall ranking. |
| **3 Commercial aspects** | Where there is an external procurement, this section outlines the potential deal. Most of this information will be produced for the Outline Business Case.

Minimum content required for this section: proposed sourcing option, with rationale for its selection; key features of proposed commercial arrangements (e.g. contract length, payment mechanisms and performance incentives); the procurement strategy with supporting rationale.

Areas that could be considered in detail are outlined below. |
3.1 Output Based Specification	Summarise the requirement in terms of outcomes and outputs; supplemented by full specification as annex.
3.2 Sourcing options	Outline the options for sources of provision of services to meet the business need – e.g. partnerships, framework, existing provider arrangements, with rationale for selecting preferred sourcing option.
3.3 Charging mechanisms	Outline the proposed charging mechanisms that will be negotiated with the providers – e.g. linked to performance and availability, providing incentives for alternative revenue streams.
3.4 Risk allocation and transfer	Summarise an assessment of how the types of risk might be apportioned or shared, with risks allocated to the party best placed to manage them, subject to achieving value for money.

3.5 Contract length	Outline scenarios for contract length and proposed key contractual clauses.
3.6 Personnel issues including TUPE	Outline personnel implications and discussions with Trade Union side where applicable.
3.7 Implementation timescales	Provide a high-level view of implementation timescales. For the Outline Business Case and Full Business Case, provide evidence of service providers' high-level implementation plans, taking into account essential considerations related to benefits realisation, risk management and control.

4 Affordability

Assessment of affordability and available funding: includes revenue implications of the public sector comparator option for PFI against main headings of PSA period, income and expenditure account, balance sheet and cash flow.
Minimum content for this section: statement of available funding and 'ballpark' estimates of projected whole-life cost of project, including departmental costs.

Areas that should be considered in detail are:

- PSA period
- income and expenditure account
- balance sheet
- cash flow.

5 Achievability

This section addresses the 'achievability' aspects of the project. Its primary purpose is to set out the project organisation and actions which will be undertaken to support procurement activity (where applicable) or detailed study with existing providers.

Minimum content for this section: high-level plan for achieving required business change, with key milestones and major dependencies (e.g. interface with other projects); outline contingency plans, e.g. addressing failure to deliver service on time, major risks identified and outline plan for addressing them; provider's plans for the same, as applicable.

Areas that could be considered in detail are outlined below.

5.1 Project roles	Set out key roles in accordance with PRINCE2 methodology.
5.2 Procurement strategy (where applicable)	Set out indicative timetable and justification for the proposed approach.

5.3 Project plan	Outline the main phases of the project plan.
5.4 Contract management	Outline Business Case: summarise outline arrangements for contract management.
5.5 Risk management strategy	Summarise outline arrangements for risk management.
5.6 Benefits realisation plan	Summarise outline arrangements for benefits management.
5.7 PIR/s and PER	Summarise outline arrangements for PIR/s and PER.
5.8 Contingency plan	Summarise outline arrangements for contingency management, such as fall back plans if service implementation is delayed.

Sourcing options: checklist

This annex provides a checklist of issues and questions to consider when deciding on a sourcing option.

Policy drivers
- What central initiatives or policies must we respond to?
- How might these constrain sourcing options?
- Are there any planned legislative or policy changes which could affect the services we require?

Business strategy
- What is the future of our core business?
- What are our corporate aims and objectives?
- Can we identify some activities as non-core?
- How clear is our strategy?

IT strategy
- How might our IT strategy constrain sourcing options?
- What is our future technical direction or strategy?
- What technology issues need to be considered?
- Are we constrained by legacy systems?

Strategic importance
- How important is the service?
- What impact does it have on the business?
- Is it core or non-core, strategic or useful?
- Can we regard the service as a commodity? Or does it differentiate us in some way?

Requirement focus	• Is the requirement oriented towards acquiring resources (for example, a number of days) which we will manage?
	• Or is it oriented towards a defined result, outcome or defined level of service performance?
	• What benefits are sought: is the emphasis on cost savings or on improvement in business value?
Demand focus	• How sure are we of future requirements?
	• With what degree of confidence can we predict demand and service volumes?
	• How do we envisage the services and our requirements might develop?
	• Are they stable or is there scope for innovation?
Purchasing approach	• Are we seeking to establish an ongoing relationship?
	• Or do we see future requirements more as a series of transactions, each of which will be completed?
Service definition	• How tightly can we specify requirements for the service?
	• Is only a loose definition possible or appropriate?
	• Will we be able to measure performance? How?
Current service performance	• How does current service performance (which may be in-house or contracted out) compare with the market as a whole?
	• What scope is there for improvement?
	• Are there any opportunities to exploit economies of scale?
	• Can this be achieved internally?
	• What is the current state of the market?

Degrees of integration	• How closely integrated is the service with others?
	• How integral to our business processes is it?
	• Could we separate it out?
	• If something goes wrong would the impact be isolated from other business activities?
Technology familiarity and maturity	• How mature is the service and the technology that underpins it?
	• How familiar are we with the technology?

Standards

D

This annex outlines which standards, methods and best practice are important and where they should be specified as a constraint.

A standard is a means of generating common understanding between customers and providers. The term 'standard' is used here to include:

- international, European and national standards which are agreed through formal standards organisations

- published specifications which have gained wide acceptance but have not reached formal status

- published methods and codes of practice in common use.

Delivery of service to the end user

The user interface is the point of contact between the user and the information system. It must meet the user's expectations and requirements. To obtain the benefits of consistency, quality and usability, standards should be specified which:

- provide effective and appropriate interfaces with the users of the systems. Organisational standards and codes of practice should be developed from OGC's guidance on user interface style guides, or other recognised best practice, and used to ensure consistent presentation to the end users of different information systems. This will lead to savings in training and operational costs of the business – for example, by increasing the mobility of staff between different functions

- enable compliance with safety, environmental and human factors (ergonomics) requirements. (Even when hardware is owned by the service provider, if it is used on the customer's premises, the customer has responsibilities for ensuring that the service meets legal requirements for health and safety.)

Development of a product

Some customers will require service providers to develop software products such as new application systems. Customers should use standards to safeguard their investment so that:

- by taking a common approach to software development the customer can:

  - choose another provider to maintain the system

  - change developer

- new applications can work with existing applications (interoperability)

- systems can operate on different computer hardware (portability). Open systems standards help to maximise the options available to the customer.

Purchasers should consider OGC's preferred methods, PRINCE2 for project management, ITIL for IT service management, and BSD SSADM for software development, which are widely used.

Managing the IT service contract

The customer is responsible for monitoring service levels and the quality of the service provided. There are no formal standards for specifying IT service provision; however, there is the IT Service Management Code of Practice – BSI:PD0005. OGC's IT Infrastructure Library gives guidance on service management and will also help in identifying the most useful information required to manage different types of service.

The IT Infrastructure Library includes guidance for service providers on how they may provide various services. There is wide acceptance of the good practice it advocates, in both the public and the private sectors.

There are internationally agreed standards for quality management that should be applied. Service providers should be required to state whether they have sought certification to these standards (EN 29000/ISO 9000/BS 5750 series) and, if so, with what result, including the scope of certification awarded.

Working with other organisations

Many organisations need to share and exchange information with others, either now or in the future, using facilities such as electronic data interchange (EDI). These may be part of the same organisation, another government department, private sector companies, the public or other governments.

The most effective way to meet this business requirement is to ensure that a service provider can share and exchange information electronically within the organisation, and with other organisations, through the use of appropriate IT standards. These standards govern both how information is exchanged and the form in which it is exchanged. They provide the business with facilities such as the exchange of revisable documents (for example, between different word processing packages) and exchange and further manipulation of more structured information such as statistics and invoices.

OGC Gateway Reviews

The Gateway Process is a Best Practice technique devised by OGC to help public sector organisations in major procurement projects. The Gateway Process is mandatory for all new high-risk projects in the civil departments of central government together with their Executive Agencies and NDPBs. This will address the recommendations of the Gershon Report on government procurement and the Cabinet Office report on *Successful IT: Modernising Government in Action*.

What is a Gateway Review?

In simple terms, a Gateway Review is a review of a project carried out at a key decision point by a team of experienced people, independent of the project team.

The Gateway Process is based on well-proven techniques used in the private sector that lead to more effective delivery of benefits together with more predictable costs and outcomes.

The Gateway Process considers the project at critical decision points in its development. These critical points are identified as gates. There are six gates during the life cycle of a project, four before contract award and the other two looking at service implementation and confirmation of the operational benefits.

For more detail, see OGC's guidance on the Gateway Process. There is also some guidance on Post Implementation Reviews, benefits management and reviewing change processes in the companion guide *How to manage Business Change*.

Gateway Review 0: strategic assessment

Gateway 0 may be applied at the start-up of either a programme or a project. The programme or project initiation process produces a preliminary justification for the programme or project based on a strategic assessment of business needs and an assessment, at a high level at this stage, of the programme or project's likely costs and potential for success.

Gateway Review 1: business justification

This first Gateway Review comes after the strategic outline case has been prepared and before any development proposal goes before a project board, executive authority or similar group for authority to proceed. The review focuses on the project's business justification. It also provides assurance to the project board that the proposed approach to meeting the business requirement has been adequately researched and can be delivered.

Gateway Review 2: procurement strategy	This Gateway Review assesses the project's viability and potential for success, and whether it is ready to invite proposals or tenders from the market. This review assures the project board that the selected procurement approach is appropriate for the proposed acquisition and demonstrates compliance with EC procurement rules. Where the organisation already has a long-term partnership arrangement, this review assesses an appropriate way forward with the existing provider.
Gateway review 3: investment decision	This Gateway Review confirms that the recommended contract decision is appropriate before the contract is signed with a provider or partner. It provides assurances on the processes used to select a provider. The review also assesses the following:

- whether the process has been well managed

- whether the business needs are being met

- that both the client and the provider can implement and manage the proposed solution

- whether contingency plans (in case of failure to deliver the service) are adequate

- that the necessary processes are in place to achieve a successful outcome after contract award.

Gateway Review 4: readiness for service	This Gateway Review focuses on whether the service solution is robust prior to delivery; how ready the organisation is to implement the business changes that occur before and after delivery; and whether there is a system for evaluating ongoing performance.
	For IT-supported business change, this review takes place after all testing, including business integration business assurance testing and contingency planning, has been completed and before roll-out or release into production.
Gateway Review 5: evaluate the in-service benefits	This last Gateway Review focuses on ensuring that the project delivers the benefits and value for money identified in the business and benefits plans.

Further information

OGC Publications

IS Management and Business Change Guides

- *How to manage Business Change*
- *How to manage Service Provision*
- *How to manage Performance*
- *How to manage Business and IT Strategies*
- *Managing Partnerships*

Other OGC publications

- *IS Strategy: process and products*
- *Achieving benefits from business change*
- *In times of radical change*
- *Managing Successful Programmes*
- *Managing Successful Projects with PRINCE 2*
- *Procurement Guidelines*
- *Supplier Financial Appraisal Guidance*
- OGC P&CD's *Guide to appointment of Consultants*
- *ITIL Service Support*
- *ITIL Service Delivery*
- *OGC Model Agreements*
- *Business System Development with SSADM*
- OGC Successful Delivery Toolkit (available online at www.ogc.gov.uk)

HM Treasury publications

For more information about OGC's products and services, call the OGC Service Desk on 0845 000 4999 or visit the OGC website at www.ogc.gov.uk

Treasury Taskforce Technical Note: Appointing and managing advisers – available on the OGC website: www.ogc.gov.uk

Index